Learn What Your Child Is Trying to Tell You—But Can't!

You think *you* have problems? Try being two. You have boundless energy, yet everyone wants you to sit still and be quiet; you're forced to share your most precious possessions with people you don't even know; and nearly every time you attempt to explore a new area or object, someone tries to stop you. To make matters worse, whether you're happy, sad, tired, or angry, you have difficulty expressing in words how you're feeling.

In this revolutionary approach to understanding a two-year-old, child development specialist Dr. Jerri Wolfe allows you to see life through your child's eyes. Each entertaining and enlightening entry identifies a common behavioral problem, presents your child's perspective to it, and then offers a variety of sensible solutions—allowing you and your child to form a bond of communication and friendship that could last a lifetime.

I'm Two Years Old!

I'm Two Years Old!

by ME

Everything Your Two-Year-Old Wants You to Know About Parenting

As Told to Jerri Wolfe

becker & mayer!
BOOKS

POCKET BOOKS
New York   London   Toronto   Sydney   Tokyo   Singapore

An *Original* Publication of POCKET BOOKS

POCKET BOOKS, a division of Simon & Schuster Inc.
1230 Avenue of the Americas, New York, NY 10020

Copyright © 1998 by Jerri Wolfe

A becker & mayer! book, Kirkland, Washington
www.beckermayer.com

All rights reserved, including the right to produce
this book or portions thereof in any form whatsoever.
For information address Pocket Books, 1230 Avenue
of the Americas, New York, NY 10020

ISBN: 0-671-00338-0

First Pocket Books trade paperback printing October 1998

10 9 8 7 6 5 4 3 2 1

POCKET and colophon are registered trademarks of
Simon & Schuster Inc.

Cover design by Patrice Kaplan, cover photo by Laurence Monneret/
 Tony Stone Images
Text design by Stanley S. Drate/Folio Graphics Co. Inc.
Interior illustrations by Ty Pollard

Printed in the U.S.A.

TO

*My daughter, Jennifer, and our friends Micah,
Nathan, Kevin, and Taylor, with whom I had the
pleasure and challenge of sharing
their second year*

and

*My husband, Mike, who still remembers
what it feels like to be two*

Acknowledgments

My heartfelt thanks to:

Karen Joslin, who thought of me when this project was first being developed.

Andy Mayer and Jim Becker, who recognized the importance of understanding the child's perspective.

My husband, Mike Johnson, for reading every word and giving me more than a few.

Ingela Hense, Linda Heard, Matt King, Debbie Patashnik, and Julie Smith, my cohorts in parenting, for walks, talks, flowers, and many hours of child care.

The dedicated parents who have attended my classes at Northwest Hospital and Overlake Hospital and who have worked with me in the Parent Education Program at Bellevue Community College. Their experiences and questions have given me a greater understanding of young children.

Contents

Introduction

I used to carry her around in a backpack, and she loved it. As she got older the backpack got too heavy for me, and she no longer desired to view the world from above but was ready to separate from me and be an active participant in the things around her. With Jennifer's changes, I was forced to change. I had been so good at keeping her clean, fed, and entertained. Now I needed to find ways to confront her refusal to wear anything but the dress her cousin Jessica gave her, her stubbornness over sharing her toys or getting in the car seat, and her appropriately used but unfortunately acquired four-letter word. It was clear some form of discipline was necessary. Being unrestrained in the car was definitely not an option, and although Jennifer's use of profanity was kind of funny it was not something we wanted to encourage.

I began considering the right thing to do and wondered: what is so special about this dress? Is the car seat uncomfortable or is being strapped in a conflict for a two-year-old whose physical skills have given her newfound freedom? How does she learn words and how will she know that some words are unacceptable? The answers to these questions led me to some interesting realizations about myself. For example, while I have several pairs of jeans in my closet there is one pair that I will go out of my way to wear. I cringe at the idea of being in a car for long periods of time, and while I am willing to share popcorn, noodles, and glue with my good friend and neighbor Linda, there are several things I am not willing to share with her or anyone. So Jennifer and I are a lot alike (although she doesn't look like me, she looks like her father); she just doesn't have the language and skills that allow her behavior to be seen as acceptable. These realizations led me to embrace a style of parenting called positive parenting. For me it means looking at what Jennifer is doing and trying to understand what she is experiencing, and what she is feeling. This approach helps me to understand that when you are two some days are just tough and that instead of being yelled at the only thing that will help is to have the one you love the most hold you and rock you.

It's not easy moving from an adult perspective into the mind and heart of a child. I have had the pleasure of spending the last year thinking like a two-year-old. I considered what it felt like to be two and hungry and tired in a grocery store, to be forced to share your most precious possessions and to be learning to use the potty. I have three degrees in families and human development, so I had a lot of academic information at my disposal. In addition I had years of learning from the parents of two-year-olds. As the child development specialist at a local community college and a parent education instructor I have had the opportunity to work with hundreds of parents. But my best teachers have been the children themselves. Jennifer and I joined a parent-infant class when she was born. The group met formally for six months, but the friendships formed have continued for years. When Jennifer was two, she and I enrolled in a parent cooperative preschool and made many more friends. These children along with the several children in our neighborhood (five were born within a two-month period) have become my teachers. Each one is unique: Jennifer will surprise you with her vocabulary, Nathan with his energy, Kevin with his sweetness, and Taylor with his determination, but each experienced being two, a time of independence, increased awareness, and incredible learning.

This book is about being two, about looking at the world through the eyes of a two-year-old. The two-year-olds in this book will tell you why they behave the way they do, how they are feeling, and what they need from us as parents. While the book is written in a child's voice, it certainly goes beyond the words and thought processes of a two-year-old. The children in this book will tell us in words we understand how to deal with the challenges we confront daily. Understanding that time is short and interruptions many, I organized this book into seventy-one short stories addressing specific issues. Choose a current challenge, and read what the child has to say. Hopefully that information will help you move beyond the frustration, anger, and desire to punish that we as parents often feel. In your spare time (sure!) read about other challenges, choosing the ones you have yet to experience. The more you understand what a two-year-old is experiencing the more tools you have for preventing problems from happening in the first place. At times two can be terrible for both parents and children, but it can also be great fun as we learn, resolve problems, and have fun together.

Activity Level (HIGH)

*I don't just like to move, I need to move.
When I'm stuck in the car seat for a long
time my body starts to feel yucky all over.
Let me out of here. I need to run,
jump, and climb.*

Outside is the best place to be. There is lots of room. I have problems when there isn't enough space for me to move. At Aunt Jessie's there is too much stuff. I knocked over a chair, got in trouble for climbing over a table (my toy was on the other side), and learned that there is no place for bouncing at her house. Aunt Jessie and you both seemed upset all the time we were there. I heard Aunt Jessie say in a strong voice to you that I was being wild. Let's not go there again.

You wished I would sit and look at books or do puzzles while you visited with Aunt Jessie. You say that I run you ragged. I'm sorry. I just have trouble doing things where you have to sit. I can only stay still for a short period of time. It is easier to sit still if I have had lots of moving. I don't have the right words but I know moving feels good. I'm good at it. Grown-ups sit too much. Doesn't your body want to move?

I NEED YOUR HELP WITH THIS. WHAT YOU CAN DO IS:

Don't try to change it, plan for it.

I am busy learning about the things around me. And I am learning how to move. I do that with my whole body. Right now I am exploring our new play structure. It is great. I am seeing how many different ways I can go down the slide, climb up, and jump to the ground. I get really frustrated when I can't go outside because it is rainy. I pound on the door because I want out. I need to be out. Could we go swimming or to the park? I like that play place with the balls, too. Could we go there?

Please make a place for me where I can play inside the house. Maybe if we moved that low table there would be room for dancing. I would like it if you would dance with me. At Jacob's house there is a basketball hoop and a slide in the house. And his mom lets us jump on his bed. She said there was only one bouncing bed in the house and it was in Jacob's room. She told us the rule was only one person jumping at a time and she had to be with us. I had so much fun jumping. I jumped really high and landed on my bottom.

Plan breaks in my day.

I have a hard time slowing down during the day. It would help if we had the same schedule every day for meals, snacks, and nap. I need some breaks and I won't take them on my own. And please give me plenty of time to unwind before bedtime. I have a hard time getting to sleep after watching TV and a really hard time after wrestling with Dad.

Protect me from real danger.

I didn't know that my car would tip over when I stood on the seat or that the swing would hit me if I ran by the swing set. I have a lot of crashes. I guess I'm so busy doing stuff that I haven't learned to think about the things around me. Maybe when I'm three I'll be able to think like that. Sometimes just moving right requires all of my concentration. But for now I need you to watch me and warn me when I do something dangerous. Instead of saying no, I listen better when you say DANGER! You will help me learn about danger by telling me why I can't run into the street, why I can't jump from the deck, and why I can't help clean the roof.

Help me when I get out of control.

Sometimes I get feeling all yucky inside and I just start to run. I just run all around and don't stop to do anything. I start to feel that way when I'm around too much noise or too many people. I am out of control and I need your help. More running will not help. I need you to help me to feel calm inside. Maybe I could blow some bubbles, take a bath, or go sit with you in our rocking chair and read a book.

Don't call me wild.

I don't mean to knock things over or break things. I didn't like it when Aunt Jessie said I was wild. I am not bad. I need to hear "You are a boy who has lots of energy, let's find a way to use it so that you and things don't get hurt." I like that, it sounds good. Tell Aunt Jessie that I'm very energetic and curious and need lots of space. Then plan for us to meet at a place where I will be able to enjoy myself, too. I know! Let's have a picnic at the park.

Take care of yourself.

I like it when you are in the playing mood. You chase me, push me on the swing, and catch me at the bottom of the slide. We have so much fun. I like to play all day. You don't want to play as much as I do. Maybe Tommy's big sister can come over and play with me, she's lots of fun. After I've had a baby-sitter, you seem to be ready to play again.

Aggression

Being a two-year-old can be pretty rough somedays.

At times I get so frustrated, like today when that boy was on the stairs of the climbing equipment at the playground. I needed to climb up and he wasn't moving, just blocking my way. So I pushed him. Then I got to the top. When I went over to the sandbox I wanted to use the yellow shovel, but that girl had it. I grabbed it, but she wouldn't let me have it at first. But when I pulled really hard, I got it. She screamed a little but then picked up the red shovel and started digging. I like to climb on the big tree stump, but I don't want anyone else on it. When Hayden comes over to climb I kick at him and he leaves. Good, now I can have it to myself. Now you say it's time to leave, no I'm not ready, I still have things to do. Don't grab me, I will hit you and kick you if you try to push me to the car.

HERE'S HOW TO WORK WITH ME ON THIS:

> Help me understand that pushing, hitting, biting, and kicking hurt.

When I was a baby I cried to let you know when I wanted something. Mostly I just wanted to eat or be held. Now that I'm two I am busy finding out all about the things around me. One thing I don't know much about is other people, especially children. Sometimes kids cry when I'm around, I'm not sure why. I am not mean or a holy terror, whatever that is. I need you to tell me, "No kicking, kicking hurts. Hayden is crying because you hurt him when you kicked him."

Keep an eye on me and step in when I get frustrated or angry.

I use my body to communicate what I want. I don't have many words, and they don't come out fast enough, particularly when I'm frustrated or angry. One minute I'm quietly playing in the backyard with my truck and the next I am pushing my friend Reed out of the red car. I want to ride. Tell me that you can see I want to ride in the red car, but that pushing is not okay. Suggest that you and I give Reed a ride in the car. Then Reed and you can push me. I learn from you, and this way you are teaching me new ways to get along. I hope when I'm three I will be able to come up with my own ideas for solving the problem but right now I need your help.

When I'm tired or hungry I really have trouble being around other kids. Let's leave the park and get something to eat or a rest before I totally lose control.

Tell me the rule is no hitting.

I feel frustrated and angry a lot. I have so many ideas about what I want to do, and they often don't go the way I want. I don't always have the words to tell you how I feel. Hitting is one way I show how angry I am. When I hit you as you drag me to the car, I need you to stop me and say, "No hitting, our rule is no hitting. Hitting hurts." Please also tell me you understand I was having a great time in the park and you know that it's hard to leave. Ask me what my favorite thing was today and tell me that we will be back soon. When I know you understand how I feel, I feel a lot better. Let's race to the car, okay?

Anger (CHILD'S)

Is being angry bad? Am I bad because I am angry? Do you love me only when I am happy?

Sometimes my whole body just starts to shake, my insides feel all yucky and I scream and hit and kick. Then it gets worse, you tell me to STOP IT! in a loud voice, take me to my room, and shut the door. It's so scary.

I FEEL THIS WAY A LOT AND I REALLY NEED YOU.
IT WOULD HELP IF YOU WOULD:

Talk to me about angry feelings.

It feels so bad and I have no control over it. Why do I feel this way? I need you to tell me that I am feeling angry. That all people feel angry sometimes. Mommy, when do you feel angry? Do you get scared, too? I feel angry a lot. Help me understand why I get that feeling by telling me why I am angry. It helps me when I hear "Tyler, you are angry because that block won't stand up" or "You are angry because we can't go to the park today."

Help me express my anger.

You tell me that I can't hit or kick or throw my toys when I am angry. What can I do? The feelings just won't go away and my body is ready to explode. Sending me to my room to calm down just makes it worse. I want to feel better, too, but I don't know how. I need you to tell me when I'm feeling angry that using my words to say what I'm feeling can help. Help me to say "I'm angry" or "You make me so mad." Show me that I can slap the floor or hit a pillow or run around the yard. I need to find a place or a way to lose my anger.

Please let me know that you won't abandon me

when I'm mad. When I get angry, you get angry, and that only makes it harder to calm down. One of us needs to be in control. When you use your calm voice and let me know you are nearby, I feel more confident that I can get through this. Sometimes what I need most is to be held.

ANGER (PARENTS')

You are driving me crazy! How many times have I told you not to do that? What's the matter with you?

Please stop. Your words hurt and scare me. Why do you yell so much? Besides, I can't even count yet, I don't know how many times you told me not to do that. I must be bad. Do you still love me?

I don't mean to drive you crazy. Being two can be really hard some days. I just have so many ideas I want to try out. I didn't remember that the milk would spill when I tipped the straw and I didn't see the water going on the floor when I was playing in the bathtub. I hope that when I am three I'll be better at knowing what will make you yell. But now your yelling confuses and scares me, I don't know what to do. I don't even know what I did.

IT WOULD HELP IF YOU WOULD:

Tell me what I did wrong.

When you say I'm driving you crazy I'm not sure what I did. It would help me if you would say "I'm angry because you spilled your milk. When you

16

play with your straw it makes the glass tip over."
Tell me how you feel and why. That will help me
learn about feelings and teach me words I can use
when I get angry. Please use your calm voice, it is
easier for me to hear. Now give me a towel and let
me help clean up, I'm good at cleaning up.

Show me positive ways to express anger.

If you scream, throw my toys, or hit me when you
are angry, I learn to do the same. I need to know
ways of showing my anger that won't get me in
trouble. Tell me that you are really angry and that
you are going to take some deep breaths, run in
place, or do some jumping jacks to make you feel
better. Maybe you need to take a time-out!

Tell me you love me.

I need to know that you can be angry at me and
still love me. When you yell I get very scared. It
helps when you say "I'm sorry I yelled at you. I
can see that my yelling frightens you. I lost my
temper when I saw the water all over the bathroom
rug. I will always love you, but sometimes the
things you do make me angry."

BABY-SITTERS

No, no. Don't leave me! NOOOOOOOOO!

It's not that I don't like Kim, I do. It's just that I get so scared when you leave. I'm afraid you won't come back. I'd like it if Kim would come over to play and you would stay. Then I could play with both of you. I just want you to stay!

*BEING SEPARATED FROM YOU IS VERY HARD FOR
ME. HERE ARE SOME WAYS YOU CAN HELP ME:*

Slow down! I need some time with you.

Get me a cookie! Read me a book! Look at me! Stop getting dressed, I want you to pay attention to me. Don't you love me anymore? I start to feel scared even before the baby-sitter comes over. You don't play with me, you're just rushing around the house, stopping only to say no. I need to know what is going to happen and that I'm still important to you. Tell me before the baby-sitter comes that you will be going out for the evening. Let me know that Kim will be fixing my favorite dinner and that she will help me with my bath and books at bedtime. Then tell me that even though I will be asleep when you get home that you will come in and tell me you love me three times. Show me that you carry my picture with you all the time, so that I am always with you, and give me a picture of you so I can feel close to you.

It is easier for me if we have some cuddle time together before Kim comes. Remind me that Kim hasn't seen my new dinosaur. Then when she gets here I can show it to her while you get dressed. Having her come a few minutes early helps me get used to her being here before you leave. When it's time for you to leave give me two big kisses and two big hugs because I'm two and tell me you love me. Kim and I will stand at the window and wave.

Listen to my sad feelings.

When you say "Stop that, you're being so silly" or "Be good and quit crying" I cry even harder. You are not listening. I am having a hard time and I need you to know. I need you to say "I know that it's hard for you when I leave, remember that I love you and I will be back." Don't be suprised if I'm still crying when you leave, I need to let all my sad feelings out.

No surprises please!

You are not Kim! I want Kim! Don't leave me with her! Help me feel comfortable with a new sitter by having her come over before she's supposed to baby-sit. Tell her about how we spend our time and what I like and what scares me. Let me show her my room, my favorite toys, and maybe she could stay and read me a book. Then we could talk about what we will do the next time she comes over.

Never, never leave without saying good-bye. How could you just leave me! The next time I have a sitter I won't start playing. I will stay attached to your leg. Even if I am busy playing I need to say good-bye. And never forget to tell me that a baby-sitter is coming. Even if I am asleep when the baby-sitter gets there I need to know. It's really frightening to wake up and not have my mommy or my daddy there.

BAND-AID OBSESSION

*Ouch, Ouch Ouch! I fell down. I need a
Band-Aid quick. I know there's no blood
but I need a Band-Aid quick! I know there's
no scrapes, I need a Band-Aid!*

I like to run really fast, go down the slide, and
drive my trike. I fall down a lot. Let's look at my
ouchies. My Band-Aids show where I got hurt, that
way I can show Joshua and Grandmom, I can show
them how brave I've been.

BAND-AIDS ARE IMPORTANT TO ME. HERE'S WHAT
I'D LIKE YOU TO DO:

Comfort me when I'm hurt.

Sometimes you think I don't need a Band-Aid
when I do. You say the Band-Aid doesn't help. I
say it does. Band-Aids are magic, they make everything better. I know. It's my body, don't fight me
on this. Band-Aids along with a special hug from
you make all the ouchies feel better. Once I have
my Band-Aid on it's easier to return to play.

Give me my own box of Band-Aids.

I am interested in my body. Why am I bleeding? Will it stop? Why does it hurt so bad? Do you ever get ouchies? I don't know how it does it but you put the Band-Aid on me and then the ouch goes away. I need a Band-Aid whenever I get a bump or scrape. I would like to have my own box of Band-Aids, then I could take care of all my ouches. Please buy me a box of yellow ones, the yellow ones work the best.

BED (FROM CRIB TO)

The things in my room are my friends,
they help me feel secure. I need to be
involved with any changes made
to my room.

I love my crib, when it's time to sleep I wiggle around until I get in the special place where my face and the rest of me feel so nice. The first thing I do when I wake up is to find Elmo, he sometimes likes to sleep at the other end of the crib. Now that I am big I don't have to wait for you to get me out of the crib, I climb out. One time I fell, but I am getting better at it. You want me to let you take me out of the crib, but I am two and this is something I can do for myself. You said soon I will be getting a big boy bed. I'm not sure what that means. I like doing things for myself and being a big boy, but I don't like surprises.

HERE'S WHAT I NEED YOU TO DO:

Let me make friends with my new bed.

I can help get the new bed ready. I can help you carry it into my room. I can hold any tools you need

24

to put in together. The sheet from my crib won't fit the big bed so we will need to go shopping. Let me pick, I want the sheets with Big Bird and Elmo on them. Elmo will be so excited. Once my sheets are on, please read Elmo and me a story. When nap time comes let me choose between the big bed and my crib, it's been so exciting getting a big boy bed, I might need the comfort of my crib to help me sleep.

Help me say good-bye.

My big boy bed is pretty good. I have slept in it now for two weeks. Sometimes I still get in my crib, but only to play. Thank you for not pushing me to use my big boy bed, I needed time to make it my own. I am probably ready for you to take down my crib, but please let me know before you do. Tell me where the crib will be going and let me say bye-bye. Good-bye old friend.

BEDTIME BATTLES

**Bedtime is the best and the
worst time of the day.**

I love it when Daddy carries me on his shoulders
upstairs to brush my teeth. We laugh so much and
then I get to pick a book sometimes two or three
to read. I like to hear my favorite stories over and
over again. But then just when I was having such
a good time you say it's lights-out time. I haven't
had enough, can't I just have one more book, I
want you to tickle me and I think I need to go to
the potty. Don't leave me, I don't want to be alone,
I need you!

You think sleep is something wonderful. You're
wrong! I think it is awful, it's dark, scary and it's
not what I want to do anyhow. I can hear you talking downstairs, I want to be with you, I'm going to
be with you, I am going downstairs to see what you
are doing.

MY IDEAS ON IMPROVING BEDTIME INCLUDE:

Spending special time with me
earlier in the day.

I love being with you, we do such fun things together. My favorites are being carried around in

27

the laundry basket, dancing, building tall towers with the blocks and then knocking them down. Many days the only time I have with you is at bedtime, so that makes that time very important to me. I try to make it go as long as possible and lots of time you get angry and yell at me. That makes me feel so bad. It's just that I need so much of you, I don't get enough time with you. I really like those days when we get some time together earlier in the day. On those days I have less trouble letting go of you at night.

Have a consistent bedtime routine.

Sometimes after we brush teeth we talk about the day or open the curtains and look at the moon. But then you say we don't have time for books. I get scared when you are in a hurry to get me in bed. I need my stories, they make me feel good and snugly. No stories and I fuss a lot. Always let me have at least one story. At the beginning of story time tell me how many books we are going to read. I don't like surprises. Then tell me you love me, give me two big kisses because I am two, and walk backward out of the room.

Calmly help me stay in my room.

Sometimes I just don't relax and go to sleep. I am alone and I'm scared. I get up to find you, I need a little reassurance that everything is okay. Then you yell at me and tell me I am to get back in my bed immediately. I cry, and you carry me upstairs and close the door. I am even more scared now.

Help me on this. Going to sleep isn't as easy as you think. It's lonely in my room. It might help if you calmly walk me back to my room and stayed with me. I'd loved it if you would lay with me, that would really help me go to sleep. The problem is that if you do lay with me until I am asleep I won't learn to go to sleep on my own. I will need you to lay with me every night. You could sit in the rocking chair. If I start to talk with you, remind me that this is sleep time and that you will stay only as long as I am quiet. If you have things you need to do and can't stay, tell me that you will come in and check on me in five minutes, just to see if I'm okay. Knowing that you'll be back I can relax and just maybe get to sleep.

BIRTHDAY PARTIES

At Maria's birthday party there was cake, and I gave Maria a present. Do I get to have a birthday?

The best part of Maria's party was the cake, it was chocolate with lots of frosting. I didn't like it when Maria's mom tried to make me close my eyes and put a tail on the donkey. I didn't want to do it. And I told her "No!" when she wanted me to walk with a ball on a spoon. I want a cake just like Maria's. Cake and presents, that's what's good about birthdays.

FOR MY TWO BIRTHDAY I'D LIKE YOU TO:

Let me help plan the cake.

I want to decide what kind of cake and what color of frosting. If you're going to make the cake, I want to help. I'm really good at dumping ingredients in the bowl and stirring. Cake smells so good when it is baking. I want my cake to be beautiful and it will be special if I can help.

Invite a few of my friends.

At birthdays everyone wears party hats. When it's my birthday I get to wear the special birthday hat. I would like Sam, Hillary, Kevin, and Maria to come. I know them well, they are my friends. Please don't invite my friends from day care, there are too many. Being the birthday girl is very exciting, and I'm likely to get overwhelmed if there are too many people.

Keep it short.

Please don't let people stay for a long time. I only have enough energy for about one hour of birthday party activity. Mostly I just want cake and presents. No games, I don't like games. When I am older I'll probably have different ideas, but for now simple is good. Simple is also easier for you.

BITING

*I wasn't planning to bite Sara,
it just happened.*

Why did I bite Sara?" I don't know, but now that you're yelling at me I'm confused and frightened. I must have done something bad, but I'm not sure what. Could you please stop yelling and hold me, I'm feeling very scared inside.

I NEED YOUR HELP, HERE'S WHAT YOU CAN DO:

Tell me what I did wrong.

I need you to tell me clearly "We don't bite people, biting hurts." Give me a piece of bread or an apple and tell me that I can bite it if I need to bite.

Give me words to express my strong feelings.

Let me know that I can use my words to tell how I feel. I need to be able to say "Stop that!" "Give it back!" and "Don't do that!" Practice them with me so that I will be more likely to remember them when I need them. When I have words I feel in control.

Anticipate the situation.

Most of the time Sara and I play well together. But sometimes I get so frustrated, like when Sara takes my doll. I need you to watch me and step in if I start to lose control. Please look for a pattern to my biting. If it happens late in the afternoon when I'm tired and hungry maybe a snack and a story will help me get enough energy to handle my frustrations.

Stay calm.

When I do bite, I need you to firmly but calmly remind me that we do not bite. If you say to me "I understand you are angry at Sara but we do not bite, biting hurts" I will be able to hear you because you acknowledged my feelings. Sara and I are both upset and your calmness will help us regain control and move beyond the bite.

Bossiness

When I was a baby I cried when I needed something to drink, then I learned the word juice. Now I have more words to let you know what I need. Get me some juice!

Ever since I was a baby you've taken care of me, getting me the things that I needed. Right now I want my crayons and some crackers. I dropped a cracker, pick it up! Mom, Mom I want some juice, mommy juice, mommmy juice. Why are you getting angry with me? I need your help, I can't get my own juice. I'm thirsty.

You say I am being bossy, but I don't know what that means. I do know it makes you angry. I don't know the words to tell you what I want the way you want me to tell you. I just tell you the best way I can.

HERE'S HOW TO WORK WITH ME ON THIS:

Teach me how to ask in my nice voice.

I don't know that there are good and bad ways to ask for things. When I say "More crackers!" tell me that when I talk to you in that voice it hurts

34

your ears and that it doesn't make you want to get crackers for me, but if I say "Mommy, please more crackers" it sounds much nicer. You will have to tell me a lot of times, it takes a while to learn new things. I want to be nice, tell me when I have used my nice voice.

Use your nice voice with me.

I hear that not-nice voice a lot—"Pick up those toys!" "Get in the car!" "Come to lunch, right now!" My ears get hurt, too! When you talk to me like that you seem mean and I feel powerless, so when I want my way that's how I talk. That's the voice you've taught me to use. I like it much better when you come and sit next to me and say it's time to pick up your toys, then you pick up the animals and I pick up the cars. I think it is easier on both of us.

Let me know you heard me.

When I don't know if you have heard me, I keep asking over and over. I can tell you don't like that either, but how will I know if you heard me? You could say "I heard you, and I'll get your juice after I get your crackers."

Help me do things for myself.

I like to do things myself. If I could reach the crayons and the paper I could get them myself. And I could get my own spoon for my cereal if I could open the drawer. My books are too high, please put them down where I can reach them. If I could get them, I wouldn't have to ask for your help.

I'm pretty used to you getting things for me (you've been doing it as long as I can remember), so sometimes I will ask you to get things I can get myself. Then you need to say "That is something you can do for yourself." I want my blanket, will you go with me to get it, I get scared when I'm by myself. Someday I'll learn to be more brave. Thank you.

CAR SEAT STRUGGLES

*Don't force me to sit in a car seat. I'm
two, I need to be free. Free to move, free
to touch and explore, and free to decide
what I want to do.*

No! I don't want to go, no car seat! NO! Maybe if
you would sit in this car seat you would understand. I need to move and I can't. I can't reach the
toys on the seat, the straps are so tight that I have
trouble moving my arms. It gets hot and when I
have my coat on I'm all cramped in. I scream and
fight with you because I want you to understand I
don't like being in that car seat.

RIDING IN THE CAR IS NO FUN. HERE ARE MY
IDEAS FOR MAKING IT BETTER:

Help me understand what safe means.

You say I must be in my car seat so that I will be
safe. Does being safe mean you are uncomfortable
and can't move? Why is not being able to move so
important? It feels bad to me. Maybe if we took my
car seat in the house we could buckle up my bear.
Then you could show me how the seat keeps the

bear from falling out or getting hurt. What being safe really means is being protected from danger. Is riding in the car dangerous? You don't have a car seat. I worry when you go in the car that it's dangerous. I think I will put my doll in the car seat, too, and protect her from danger.

Show me that the seat belts you use are made to protect grown-ups from danger. When I get bigger I will get to wear one like that. Tell me that the rule in our family is that everyone is buckled in before the car moves. We do that because we love each other and always want to be safe. Tell me that it's so important to be buckled up that it is a law. Let me be in charge of checking that everyone has buckled up, then I will give you the okay to start the engine.

Even though I know what *safe* is I will resist getting in the car seat. Is "everyone wears their belt" a one-time rule or all the time? If you don't wear yours or you let me ride without mine one time, then I will not be sure when we have to follow the rule. When I start to resist, give me the choice of getting in myself or having you put me in. I'll need a minute to decide. When we are talking about where we are going and what I get to do I sometimes even forget about the car seat problem and just get in. It would be a lot easier to forget about if it was more comfortable. I have had this seat since I was a baby, can you make it feel better?

Making riding in the car more fun.

When I get tired of being in the car or can't reach a toy I wiggle out of my car seat. Wow, do you ever get mad. Please put my toys where I can reach them. It's also better when I can listen to one of my music tapes, it gives me something to think about. And I like to play games with you, like see who can find a yellow car. If we are going to be in the car for a long time, stop so I can get out and run. I look forward to the park on the way to Grandma's house, she lives so far away.

CHORES

*I'm not ready to do chores on my own but
I really like to help you. I can match socks,
dust, put the place mats on the table,
and put dirty clothes in the hamper.*

I am interested in the things around me. Today I watched you sort the clothes in piles and put some of them in the washing machine. Let me put the soap in! I like watching the soap get all mixed up with the clothes. Next the clothes go in the dryer. When they come out they are all warm. I like to hold them close to me. Can I help? I can put all the socks in one pile and all the underwear in another. Getting the clothes clean is important and I feel good when I help.

Sometimes you say "Thank you, but I don't need any help right now, go and play with your train." You'd rather do it yourself. When I help it takes longer and sometimes I don't get it quite right. Okay, I'll play with my train but I really want to help. There will probably come a time in the future when I won't be so eager to help. Are you sure you don't want to take advantage of my helpfulness now?

*I LIKE TO HELP. HERE'S WHAT I WOULD LIKE YOU
TO DO:*

Encourage me to help.

Instead of no, thank you, I'd like to hear "Sure. I'd love to have your help." What grown-ups do is important and when I get to do those things, too, I feel important. Tell me where dust comes from, show me how to dust, and give me my own special dust rag. After I'm done thank me for helping and tell me I'm becoming an A-number-one duster. I'd like that. But don't make dusting my regular job. I'm still learning and I work best when you are with me and when I choose to help. Some days I will be too busy building a tower with my blocks or playing under the table to help with dusting.

By including me in the caring for the house I learn that we all have a part in keeping things nice. There are a lot of chores we can do together. Gradually I will become good enough to do some tasks on my own. But right now I enjoy being with you. If instead you do it all, I will learn to expect you to do all the work. Then when you ask me to help when I'm older I will refuse. Why should I do your job? The choice is yours. Spend the extra time with me now or hassle with me about tasks when I'm older.

Let chores be fun.

Why do you grumble about doing chores. Are they bad and something to be avoided? I'm confused. I think doing chores is fun. I love to wash the plastic containers in a sink all full of bubbles and then rinse the bubbles off. You are in charge of drying, okay? I have a lot of fun doing outside chores, too. I like to use my bucket to collect fir cones, and to use my new shovel to dig holes for the flowers. And it's so much fun to wash the car. You let me squirt your feet with the water and you squirt mine, but don't spray me in the face, I don't like it. Sometimes I get all wet. When we raked leaves, we made a huge pile and then jumped into it. Let's do that again.

CLOTHING CHOICES

I want to wear the dress cousin Jessica gave me. I like it because it has a sparkling unicorn on it, I can put it on myself, and it feels good.

I don't want to wear those pants and that shirt. I don't care if I wore my Jessica dress yesterday. I don't care if it is in the wash. And I don't care if it is cold outside. I want to wear my Jessica dress!

You make getting dressed such a struggle. I am two not a baby anymore. I need to help decide what I'm going to wear. When I was a baby I didn't pay much attention to clothes. You dressed me the way you liked. Now I think about my clothes and I want to wear clothes that I like. Clothes that are me. I am not you, I need to find my own style. I like clothes that are soft, clothes that are my favorite colors, and clothes that have animals or flowers on them. You want me to wear those pants. I won't! They don't feel good.

WHAT I WEAR IS VERY IMPORTANT TO ME. HERE'S HOW TO WORK WITH ME ON THIS:

Let me wear my Jessica dress.

I like my cousin Jessica so much. I'm so excited that she gave me her special unicorn dress and that

43

I am big enough to wear it. Why does it matter if I wore it the day before? Why do you and other people care if I wear it two days in a row? I want to wear it every day right now. If I can't wear my dress during the day, then let me wear it in the evening or after bath over my pj's. Yeah, I like that idea, I could sleep in my Jessica dress.

I need to know that the reason my dress is in the wash is that it is dirty. That washing it helps to keep it looking nice. Let me help wash my dress. I can put the soap in. I want to get it nice and clean.

Let me help pick my clothes.

I have favorite clothes, which I like to wear, don't you? I don't like having important decisions like what I'm going to wear made for me. You decide what you're going to wear every day, don't you? But I will need your help. I still have a lot of learning to do about clothes. It would help if you would put away my shorts now. When I see my shorts I want to wear them, they are so comfortable and they remind me of warm weather. Too bad it isn't warm outside. If I can't see them I won't likely think of them and make a fuss. Let's look out the window and talk about the weather for today. Today it is cold and rainy so I will need to wear warm clothes. Give me two or three choices of warm clothes to wear. Don't give me too many things to choose from, I get confused.

Please don't buy me any more dresses with ties in the back. They look pretty, but they hurt when I sit back. Sometimes clothes just don't feel good. I know you want me to look pretty for Grandma's birthday party but I won't wear that yellow dress. Can I have another choice?

CRIES EASILY

Don't call me a crybaby, I'm not a baby!
It's just that there are a lot of things
that make me cry. I don't know why,
it just happens.

Why do you get so angry when I cry? Why do you tell me to "stop that"? I can't stop, and yelling at me doesn't help, it just makes me scared. When things go wrong, like when Owen took my shovel or when my airplane got broken, I felt so bad inside all I could do was cry. I cry when I fall and scrape my knee, bump my head on the bed, or step on a toy. Steven doesn't cry when he falls down, he just gets back up. My ouchies hurt so bad, why don't Steven's? I really cry hard when you use your mad voice at me when I spill my juice. That voice really scares me. After I'm done crying I feel a lot better.

Sometimes I cry when other people get hurt, like when that girl fell down at the park. I can feel her pain, why can't you? When you are happy it makes me feel all good inside, and when you're sad I can feel that, too. I feel a lot of things. I don't know why, I guess I was just born that way.

PLEASE DON'T ASK ME NOT TO FEEL. WAYS YOU CAN HELP ME INCLUDE:

Teach me about feelings.

I don't always understand what makes me cry, it just happens. I need to hear that feelings are inside of me. I need to know that it's okay to feel happy, excited, scared, and sad. Tell me that everyone has feelings and that my body feels things very strongly. That not everyone feels things as strongly as I do. People who are as sensitive as I am care very deeply for others and make great friends.

Acknowledge my feelings.

When I fall down and start to cry, please come over and ask me where I hurt. Then ask me if I need a hug. Sometimes one hug makes the hurt go away, but sometimes I will need a Band-Aid. Band-Aids really help, even when the skin is not broken. Beware, if you make a really big fuss over my ouchies, I will have ouchies more often. I like the attention. Reassure me, but help me learn how to deal with being hurt.

I need to know the words for feelings. When you say "I see you are angry because Owen took your shovel" I learn the word *angry*. Then the next time Owen takes one of my toys I might be able to say "You make me angry" instead of crying.

Use your quiet voice when you need to correct me.

I don't want to misbehave. There are just so many things I don't know. When I'm doing something wrong, come close to me and tell me without your mad voice. The mad voice gets me so upset inside that I forget what you told me. If I don't listen you can use a strong voice, but don't shriek. When you shriek you sound out of control.

Tell me how you are feeling.

I can feel when you are feeling bad, but I don't know why and it scares me. It would help if you told me "Today I'm feeling sad because I heard that a friend of mine is sick." I don't need to know too much, just a little really helps.

Dawdling

*Why are you always in a hurry? I don't like
it when you tell me to hurry up.*

In the morning, I'm busy, I don't want to go to
wherever you are going. I want to stack my blocks
and see them when they fall. I want to make a path
with the blocks and drive my cars on it. I want to
open and close the block that works like a door and
put animals through it. There are so many great
things to do with blocks.

When we're on a walk I want to walk in the
leaves and hear them crunch under my feet. I also
want to pick them up, drop them, and kick them.
It's hard to get all that done when you are in a
hurry. Even when I'm trying to hurry I often see
something interesting that needs to be checked
out.

HERE IS HOW TO WORK WITH ME ON THIS:

Give me time to play.

I need blocks of time where I can play without interruptions. I have so many ideas, and I want to do
them all. When you stop me before I'm finished

with "Get your coat on right now—we're leaving," I get angry and protest very loudly.

It's hard for me to walk with you. I see so many things that I want to explore. (I am a lot closer to the ground, remember.) Take me outside to explore without being in a hurry. If you really need to get somewhere either put me in the stroller or carry me. I just don't move at your pace.

Help me change my focus.

I get very involved in playing. Sometimes when you yell at me to start picking up my toys from across the room, I don't even hear you. I'll need a little forewarning before I can stop what I am doing. You could say "Honey, in five minutes it will be time to get ready to leave." Then sit down next to me and ask which animal you can put through the door. We could even set the door on the animal container and put them away through the door. After we're finished, walk with me to my coat. If you leave me at the toys to do it on my own I'm likely to see something else to do.

Day Care Drop-Offs

I am not acting like a baby! A baby doesn't know that his mommy and daddy are separate from him and that they can leave him and never come back!

Even though I love the big climbing toy and the rocking horses at the day care center I get really scared when you leave. So scared that I plead, "Please don't go." I cry because I'm feeling very upset and then I beg for three more kisses and then five more kisses because I'm trying to get you to stay longer. Pleading doesn't seem to work but begging for kisses always gets me a few more minutes with you. After you leave I cry for a few more minutes and then I start to feel better. I am slowly learning that I can handle being away from you, and that when you leave you are not gone forever and that you will be back after nap time.

I HAVE A LOT OF TROUBLE WHEN YOU LEAVE. IT WOULD HELP IF YOU WOULD:

Feel good about leaving me.

Why are you upset, Mommy? Is there something wrong? Is there something wrong with this place?

I get upset when you are upset. Please find a place for me where you know I will be well cared for. A place where the grown-ups like two-year-olds, are really nice, and there are lots of fun things to do. When you are happy it is easier for me to feel confident that I can make it without you. Isn't that what you want?

Give me a short and very sweet good-bye.

Every day is different. Some mornings you just walk me to the door and say good-bye, other mornings you come in the room with me and we look at all of my paintings before you leave, and sometimes you go and talk to the teacher and leave without even saying good-bye. I'm never sure what's going to happen. It would help if we did the same thing every day. Routines help me to feel secure. I would like it if we had time enough every day to put my things in my cubby, walk into the room, and say hello to the teacher. You could ask me what I am going to play with first today. And then tell me it is time for you to go. Please don't say "I'm leaving now, okay?" because I really don't have a choice, do I? Next ask me if I want two hugs and kisses or three hugs and kisses today. I want four kisses and four hugs! Lastly, say good-bye, you love me bunches and gobs, and walk out the door.

If I plead and cry, tell me that you understand I don't want you to go. Tell me that you love me and that you will be back. If I beg for more kisses tell me that you and I will have four more kisses when you get back, and then go. The longer you stay the more upset I get and the longer it takes me to start to feel good after you leave. When I am very upset it helps if a teacher walks over to the window and helps me wave good-bye.

DRESSING

You say it's time to get dressed,
I say only if you can catch me,
and even then I will fight you.

I like my pj's, they're so nice and cuddly. Why do I have to put on day clothes? Getting dressed hurts. I don't like things being pulled over my head, pulled up my legs, tucked in around my middle, and put on my feet. I don't like having things done to me.

INSTEAD OF STRUGGLING, WHY DON'T WE
TRY THIS:

Teach me to dress myself.

I like to do things myself. Lay my shirt out for me and show me how I can put my shirt on myself. Make sure it is a shirt with a big neck. It doesn't feel good when the shirt pulls down over my nose and my ears. I can put my own pants on if you hold them out and have me put one leg in at a time. Then I can pull them up. I like sweatpants the best, they are soft and easy to put on. Hooray! I did it. Learning to get dressed takes effort, so please plan lots of time. I can't be rushed.

Make getting dressed fun.

When I get up in the morning we always have a nice warm hug. I like that. Then you set me down and I go play with my toys. Once I'm playing I don't want to stop to get dressed. Maybe it would work better if I got dressed before I started to play, when I'm still a little sleepy. We could play a game. I like it when you put the shirt over my head and say where is Tyler. Then we giggle and we pull the shirt over together, and you say there you are and give me a big kiss. I think it's really funny when you play "this little piggy went to market" with my toes. Then blow in my sock, and put it on fast while it is still warm. I like playing games with you, it makes it a good morning.

Eating Out

I like to eat at the chicken place. They have dinosaur chicken, crayons, and good cookies.

When we eat at the chicken place I don't have any problems. But at that noodle place I had real trouble. We had to stand to wait for a table, and there were people too close to me. You tried to make me sit in the high chair, I won't sit there, I'm a big boy. The chair was too low, but I sat in it anyway. I was so hungry, I need my food. While I waited and you talked, I started dipping my spoon in the water to get a drink. Only a little water spilled. You told me to stop, I did, but then I didn't have anything else to do so I got another sip. This time a lot of water spilled. The food finally came, but there was sauce on my noodles, I like my noodles without sauce. I won't eat it. I don't like that place. I don't think you had a good time either.

MY IDEAS FOR HAVING A GOOD TIME
EATING OUT ARE:

Pick a child-friendly restaurant.

The chicken place is my favorite place to eat. Not only do they have my kind of food, but I always get to sit in a booth by the window, and they bring you some chewy bread right away. I even get to color on the table because it is covered with paper. The workers smile a lot and don't seem upset if something gets spilled. When we go somewhere I feel comfortable, I learn that eating out can be fun and the food can be good, too. I can also learn the different rules for different places.

Be prepared.

If we go somewhere other than Fran's, make sure we go before it gets crowded. When we eat at home it never takes this long. I have trouble waiting, and all the noise bothers me. It would help if you brought some crackers for me to snack on while I'm waiting for my food and some toys to play with. It really helps if you color with me or play with my toys with me. I seem to get in the most trouble before the food comes and no one is giving me any attention. It's hard, too, when I'm done eating and you're still eating or talking. Hurry up, I'm done, it's time to go.

EATING (PICKY)

You can't force me to chew and swallow.
I will decide what I will eat.

I really do like food, it's just that you won't leave me alone when it's mealtime. You put huge amounts of food on my plate and then bug me to try the strawberries, to drink my milk, and tell me not to fill up on crackers. I would like a chance to sit and look at, touch, and smell my food. I need to decide what I'm going to eat. Some days I am not very hungry and other days I could eat all day. Noodles are my favorite food right now and I want them at every meal. They just feel and taste good and I like eating something I can count on.

I can tell what I eat is really important to you. But I'm two, and two-year-olds don't like to be pushed around. I'm in the process of becoming independent.

HERE ARE SOME WAYS YOU CAN WORK WITH ME ON THIS:

> Provide a variety of healthy foods
> and then back off.

I may not eat everything you think I should eat in one day to be healthy, but if you watch my eating over a week you'll find that I do pretty good. Trust me on this. What I need from you is to lighten up and provide me with a favorite food, like noodles, you know I will eat and some other foods. And I would appreciate it if my foods were easy to eat. I like things that are cut up so that I can pick them up with my fingers. I especially don't like things with runny sauce on them. YUCK.

I can tell you get pretty frustrated with me. Some days I just don't feel like eating what you fixed, even if it is my favorite. Maybe you could offer me one other thing that's simple, like cold cereal, then I could choose. If I wouldn't eat either I guess I'll just have to wait until the next mealtime.

I need more than three meals a day.

Even when I eat a good breakfast I sometimes get hungry before lunchtime. My stomach doesn't seem to hold enough food to get me to the next meal. When I get hungry I start to bug you for cookies and stuff like that. But when I eat too close to dinnertime then I'm not hungry for dinner. It would help if I could have a couple of regular snacks during the day, but not too close to mealtimes.

EMPATHY

*Why am I so self-centered? Well,
it's because I'm two.*

Stop, you can't take the Play-Doh from Tommy,
look you have enough to play with right here." "No!
Reed, you can not push Quinn out of the way. It is
his turn to go down the slide." You wonder why day
after day I have problems when I'm around other
children. I am just beginning to learn about what I
can do, what I like, and how my actions affect other
people. I don't understand my own feelings, let
alone the feelings of others. I get yelled at a lot but
I'm not always sure why.

I CAN LEARN KINDNESS. HERE ARE SOME WAYS
YOU CAN HELP ME:

> Help me understand how the
> other child feels.

I don't always know that a child is crying because
of something I have done. I only know that I
wanted to go down the slide, and I did. I need you
to tell me "Look at Quinn. He is crying because you
pushed him and hurt him. How do you think he

60

feels?" Talk to me about feelings. Remind me how I felt when I got pushed and fell down. Then when we're reading a story or watching TV ask me how I think the people are feeling. Is the little boy happy that there is a monster in the closet or scared?

Be sure and tell me that in our family we don't push, bite, or hit other people. All of these things hurt, and we don't hurt other people. And we won't accept other people hitting or pushing us. We have better ways to deal with problems.

Be sensitive to my feelings.

It helps so much when you cuddle with me when I'm sad or give me a special mommy kiss to make my ouchies go away. When you listen to me, and treat me kindly, it makes me feel good. I like it so much that I will try to make other people feel good when they are sad. Daddy, would you like to cuddle with my blanket? Maybe it will make you feel better.

Involve me in caring for others.

I like it when we do things for other people. Yesterday we surprised Daddy by getting him a pear. We shopped for just the right pear. It was exciting to think about choosing something to make him happy. He loves pears, and he shared it with me. Today we are making pumpkin muffins and taking some to my friend Penny. She is always so nice to me. She lets me walk around her garden, and once she let me have a plant to put in my garden. But this time I have something for her. I can't wait to give her some of the muffins we baked. I love Penny's smile.

Fear of Animals

*I don't like animals, not snakes, not
spiders, and definitely not dogs.*

When I see Jason's dog I grab on to your leg and start to cry. You tell me not to be silly, that Cosmo won't hurt me. You are not listening, I am afraid! Cosmo is bigger than me and he barks and he could knock me over and he might eat me like animals do on TV. We don't have a dog and I'm not used to them. I get even more afraid when you don't protect me. Please, please don't force me to go near that dog or any dog.

HERE'S HOW YOU CAN HELP ME:

Give me a sense of control.

I am not a baby anymore and it is very important for me to have control over the things in my life. What makes dogs so scary is that I don't know what they're going to do. I can remember when Suzy's dog jumped up on me and licked me on the face. Yuck. It was very bad and scary.

If I am going to be around animals I'm going to need to feel in control. How about if we start with plastic animals? I could play with them. They can't hurt me. Using a stuffed dog, you could teach me how to pet a dog. I love to read books. Let's read some books about dogs, like dogs and children being friends and dogs who save the day. Even with all these I will still need some time before I'm ready to approach a dog. Don't hurry me. Show me that you are not afraid and pet the dog. I will decide if I am feeling brave. It would help if it was an adult dog that is used to children, puppies wiggle around and jump up too much.

Teach me safety skills.

I am not a fraidy cat. I think being a little afraid of animals is a good thing. You wouldn't want me to just play with any snake, spider, or dog, would you? Some can really hurt you. I know, I saw a snake bite a man on TV. How will I know which animals are okay and which are not? You need to tell me to never go near an animal without a grown-up around. If I do decide to go near Cosmo I need to know to approach him slowly, that dogs get scared when children move quickly and also when they use loud voices. Show me how I am to put my hand out so the dog can smell me, and once he has I can pet him gently on the head behind the ears or under the chin, but never by his eyes. And don't pull his tail or tug his ears, dogs hate that, too.

FRIENDS

I like being with Michelle, she
and I are both two.

When I see my friend Michelle I get so excited I run up and hug her. Sometimes my hugs make her cry, but after we both get up off the ground we go over to her sandbox and dig. She uses the blue bucket and shovel and I use the yellow. Last time we played we had some trouble over who would use the red ones, but that isn't an issue today. I am building a mountain, I watch Michelle as I build and see that she is using her shovel to dig a hole. Maybe I'll dig a hole when I'm finished with my mountain.

Since I'm only two it can be hard at times for me to be with other kids. I'm so busy doing what I want to do that I can't think of how someone else feels. Playing with other kids is kind of like learning to walk, there are a lot of bumpy times and it takes a lot of practice.

I NEED FRIENDS, HERE'S HOW YOU CAN HELP:

Find a consistent friend for me.

I like playing at places like the park, and I check out the kids who are there, but my favorite thing is

to play with a child I know. I get all excited when
you tell me Kevin or Michelle is coming over. I
know them, we have played before. I particularly
like being with Michelle, she likes to play in the
sand like I do and she likes to run around the yard.
I have learned that she doesn't like sand in her face
and that she won't let me touch her blue bucket
and shovel, they're her new ones.

Arrange short play dates for me.

I get excited when a friend comes over. We do so
many things, eat crackers, play with my toys, play
peekaboo with you in the playhouse. I get tired
pretty fast and then I start having trouble. Play
dates start out good but sometimes end bad. I don't
like that bad feeling.

And don't have more than one child come over,
two is too many for me.

Meet at a neutral sight.

When I feel a strong need to protect my toys it's
no fun to have a friend over. I do much better at
the park. So instead of Michelle coming to my
house, or me going to hers (she also is having a
problem with sharing) let's meet at the park. We
can bring lunch and make it a picnic, yum.

"GIMMES"

I want the pink pony. I love little ponies, and this one sparkles. I am holding on to it tightly so you must let me keep it. No! I will not put it back.

I love toys, they are very important to me. Having lots of toys—my kind of toys, animals, dolls, things that sparkle and shine—makes me feel good. Why can't I have the pink pony? It would make me so happy.

You take me shopping and we buy things. The store has so many neat things, at times I want everything. Don't you ever feel that way? Sometimes you buy me toys and other times you say no. Why can't I have all the toys I want?

I'M CONFUSED. I NEED YOU TO TELL ME ABOUT MONEY.

Explain where you get money and how our family uses it.

It looks to me like all it takes to buy something is a gold card or a piece of paper you write on. If I had a gold card of my own I could buy everything

I want. How can I get my own gold card? I need you to tell me that you go to work to earn money. Then our family takes the money it earns and pays for the things we need like food, water, and heat. There is enough money to pay for the things we need but not enough to buy everything we want.

Make a list.

That doll on the TV looks so neat. I want one and I want you to know it. Please listen. Let's make a list of all the toys I want. We can hang it on the refrigerator. Then when we have some money for toys you could pick something off the list.

It is really hard for me to go into a toy store and just look at toys. Why are we going to the toy store if we aren't buying toys? Toys are so important to me that I just can't control the wants. If you have to take me to the store tell me what's on your shopping list. I can help you find the right Barbie for cousin Jessica's birthday. Maybe today we will have enough money for that pink sparkling pony? Maybe? Yes!

GROCERY SHOPPING

*Not again. Why are we going to the store
again? I don't like the grocery store, too
many bad things happen there, they are
not good places for two-year-olds.*

At first, it seems like a perfect place, lots of room,
things of different colors, shapes, and sizes to explore and learn about. But when I try to do the
same things that the grown-ups are doing—like
grabbing apples, smelling peaches, and putting
things in the cart—I only get told no. There are so
many things I see I want, why are you the only
one who gets to put things in the cart? Getting the
groceries takes so long, and now we have to wait in
line, if only I could have that candy right there in
front of me I would feel a lot better. How can you
expect me to sit quietly in the cart while so much
is going on around me? I'm two. I get so frustrated,
all I can do is scream. In fact I can scream really
well, and it does get your attention, and that of lots
of other people, too.

MY IDEAS FOR MAKING GROCERY SHOPPING
EASIER ON ME AND YOU ARE:

Leave me at home.

I'd rather stay home and play outside with my trike and my shovel than go to the store. I'm busy doing things, at the store I get in trouble if I do things. Being home is much better. It's really hard for me to go shopping when I'm hungry, I keep smelling good things, like cookies, but you won't let me have any. When I'm low on energy any frustration causes me to start screaming.

When you can't leave me home, please don't yell at me if I start to have trouble. Even when I'm rested the store can be difficult for me, shopping takes too long. So please if I have to go shopping let's go when the store is not busy, so we can get out more quickly.

Oh, and if I start running down the aisle tell me that I can either sit in the cart or walk next to you. If I continue to run down the aisle I guess I don't have the self-control to stay next to you. Put me in the cart and give me something to do. Maybe I could snack on some raisins or an apple. Sometimes it helps to get away from all the people and noise for a few minutes. Tell me that you know shopping is hard, give me a hug, and then hold me while I get in control. Then tell me what we have to do next, and let's work together to get out of the store as quickly as we can.

Let me help.

You have told me that I'm not to run in the aisles, not to touch anything, and not to use my loud voice. What can I do? I would like it if you would let me help make the grocery list. I could look in the refrigerator with you to see if we need cheese, milk, and yogurt. We could check to see if we need any crackers or cookies. Then you could tell me that I am in charge of getting the cheese and the crackers. I love to be in charge of things. I also like to put things in the cart, visit the lobsters in the big tank, help pick a special treat for Dad, and put apples in the bag. I liked it when you showed me there were four different kinds of apples. We decided to try a new one, I can't wait to get home and see what it tastes like. Maybe the checker will put it in a special bag just for me. After a successful shopping trip, I like it when you tell me that I am a good shopper and that you appreciated my help.

If you're in a hurry let me know. Tell me that today we are going to hurry in and get just two things from the store. We don't have time to visit the lobsters, only to get two items and get in line. Tell me what two things we are getting and ask me to help you remember them. I can tell you get frustrated when the line is long. Maybe we could talk about what we are going to do when we get home or maybe just hug. Hugs really help me when I'm frustrated.

Hair Washing

You think I'm fussing about hair washing for no reason. But there is a really important reason. Hair washing feels bad.

I like to play in water, to pour water in my water-wheel and to make rain with my bucket with the holes in the bottom. I like to run through the sprinkler, the little sprinkler only. I don't like the big sprinkler because I don't like to get water in my face. That's one of the bad things about hair washing. Water gets in my face and sometimes in my eyes. It stings when it gets in my eyes. Another bad thing about hair washing is the soap, it smells.

Even when my hair is all dry it still smells like that soap. And hair washing takes too long. No hair washing!

SOME WAYS TO WORK WITH ME ON THIS ARE:

Keep the water and soap
out of my face.

My friend James gets to wear a kind of hat (his mom said it was called a visor) on his head when he gets his hair washed. It keeps things from getting in his face. I want one just like James has. And I would like it if you would get a shampoo that didn't sting or smell. Hair washing doesn't hurt at James's house.

Make hair washing fun.

I am busy and I don't like taking time out from playing in the bath to wash hair. It would be fun if you used your Mickey Mouse voice and I can pretend Micky is washing my hair. Or we could play beauty shop, and I could soap my hair all up and make fancy hairdos. Could we get a special mirror that wouldn't break for the bath? I could look at myself that way. Maybe one of my dolls would like to come in the bath for a shampoo and fancy hairdo.

Hey, how often do I really need to wash my hair? Does my hair need to be washed as often as my body? Could we wash one day and then skip the next day?

Holiday stress

I don't like this food, I want cheese. Please don't let that lady kiss me! What is a holiday, anyway?

Why are we always hurrying to go somewhere? I don't want to go shopping and look at the pretty decorations! Why are you so grumpy? Even finding a place to park makes you angry. I want to be home, where it is quiet and I can take my nap in my own bed with my bear and my blanket. I don't want to go to Aunt JoAnn's for dinner! And I don't want to wear these clothes, they make me feel itchy. There are too many new things for me. I get tired and scared. Everything is new and different. I like ordinary days. I understand them.

HOLIDAYS ARE HARD ON ME. SOME WAYS YOU CAN MAKE THEM BETTER INCLUDE:

Don't disrupt my routine.

When I am rested I have the energy for new things. So, please plan outings during my good times, not during nap times. I have real trouble when I don't get to eat and sleep at the right time.

And don't try to force me to eat food I don't know. Having food that I like tastes good and makes me feel good, too!

Protect me from strangers.

No I won't give a hug to Aunt Marie. I want only my parents that close to me. Hugs are only for you. You don't hug strangers, do you? Why do people I don't know want to kiss and hug me? I don't like it! I don't know Aunt Marie, she smells funny, and I don't know Aunt Claire and Uncle Tom. And please don't make me sit on Santa's lap, he is really scary.

Spend lots of quiet time with me.

When we are at home you tell me you are busy. When we go visiting you talk only to the other grown-ups and not me. Don't you love me any-more? I need you to be with me. I can help you put up the decorations and I love to bake cookies. But most of all I need quiet time where we can sit and talk and rock.

IMAGINARY FRIENDS

*Ashley is a good friend, she always wants
to do what I want to do, she never gets
angry, and she's never in a hurry.*

I have a new friend, her name is Ashley. She is
a princess. She and I are both two. Ashley knows
everything, is very strong, and is not afraid of anything. Ashley likes to play in my room, go for car
rides with me, and sometimes when I'm scared at
night she sleeps right next to me.

I really like my time with Ashley, she always
comes when no one else can play. It's nice to have
a new friend. Now I have lots of friends to play
with. This morning Ashley and I fed all my stuffed
animals, took turns going down the slide, and
stacked the blocks really high.

You seem a little confused about Ashley. Maybe
if you knew more about her you wouldn't be
concerned. Don't worry, there is nothing wrong
with me.

THINGS TO KNOW ABOUT ASHLEY AND ME:

Only I can see her and she
only talks to me.

I will let you know when Ashley needs something.
When she is visiting, please make Ashley feel wel-

come by saying hello and asking about her. You are very nice to my other friends, fixing them snacks and letting them go with us to the zoo. Ashley likes those things, too, and I like her to be with me. Never say anything bad about Ashley, it hurts her feelings and makes me really angry. Let me decide what is best for Ashley. She is my special friend, remember.

Ashley helps me solve problems.

There are so many things to learn when you are two. Because Ashley is two, she knows how I feel and we can talk about problems. Ashley is really brave, she checks under the bed for monsters before we go to sleep. And when you leave me at day care I don't feel as sad if she is with me. She reminds me that you always come back. Don't worry, she is really good, and she's always there to help me when I need her. It's great to have a friend like Ashley.

INDEPENDENCE

Me do it! Let me do it! No, myself! I want to do it! Someday I will be able to do almost everything myself. That will make your job much easier.

When I was a baby I had to figure out when I was hungry, wet, and sick and let it be known. I had to have your help. Thank you, you have taken such good care of me. Now that I am comfortable moving around on my own it's time for me to start learning to take care of myself. I feel so good when I do something myself. Today I buttoned my sweater (the one with the big buttons), washed my hands, and put jam on my toast, even if it was messy. I also like to be first when we walk to the bathroom for teeth brushing and to push the button whenever we come to an elevator. This is so important to me that I scream and make a huge fuss when you push the elevator button instead. Sometimes I'm slow, but let me do the things I can, at least let me try.

LEARNING TO BE INDEPENDENT IS HARD WORK.
HERE ARE SOME WAYS YOU CAN HELP ME:

Allow lots of time.

I do not brush my teeth or put on my socks as quickly as you do. I am just learning. Can you remember trying to learn something new? Sometimes you get in a hurry and try to do these things for me. I want to do them myself. I do like it when you stay near me when I am working on something. Sometimes I get really frustrated because I can't get it to go right, like when I was trying to get my coat on. I liked it when you asked me if I would like you to show me the way you learned to put your coat on when you were little. Some jobs I'll finish on my own, that makes me feel good. Other times I'll want you to help me finish. I don't always know when.

Make things easier for me.

It's hard to wash your hands when the sink is so high. And I can't reach the soap or the towel. I could put on my panties and my socks but I can't get them, the drawer is too hard to open. I wish grown-ups were the same size as kids. Then things would be easier.

Please be patient.

Sara opened the door, I wanted to do it! You turned the page on the book, let me do it! I want to push the cart at the grocery store! If you really have a good reason why I can't, please show me another way I can help. Maybe I could pick out three apples and two boxes of noodles. I tried and tried to ride Zach's trike, but it's just too big. So many things are so hard. I get so frustrated all I can do is scream. But I will keep on trying. How will I know if I can do it if I don't try? You do want me to learn, don't you?

After working hard at being independent I sometimes need a break. Then I will insist on being carried, having you dress me, and prepare my toast. Do you ever just want someone to take care of you? It feels so good. Doing things for yourself is good but so is having someone you can count on.

Language

You speak better than I do. It is easy for you. You must be smart.

Learning to talk is frustrating. I try to say *dog* but it comes out *gog*. I try to tell you I want some water and you hear I gant some gater. You just smile, shake your head, and continue to fix dinner. You didn't hear me I gant some gater!

SOME WAYS YOU CAN HELP ME INCLUDE:

Stop! Listen to me.

There are so many things I want to tell you, but you are not a good listener. A lot of the time you don't let me finish, you start to talk before I'm done. Sometimes you just look at me for a minute, smile, and then turn away. How am I going to learn to talk if I don't have someone to talk to? I want you to come and get down by me so we're eye to eye. I want to talk.

Listen and add. Please don't correct.

I am doing the best I can. I don't like it when you tell me no, it's not *gog* it's *dog* and try to make me

84

say *dog*. What I would like you to do instead is say, "Yes, I see Erin's dog, Jamie, over by the tree." I need to hear the words correctly, and that doesn't make me feel bad.

Talk to me, I am learning words from you.

Before I can use a word I have to hear it. I spend a lot of time with you and I like it when you tell me what you are doing. I learn best when I hear and see and even taste or smell something. I learn lots of words when we cook together. You told me you were stirring the batter and then I got to do it. You let me fill the cup up to the top with sugar and then you put some sugar on my hand for me to taste. It was really good. The vanilla smelled good, but you said it tasted yucky, so we didn't taste it. Making cookies is so much fun.

One of my other favorite ways to learn words is to look at books. Right now I like the story about the bear and the book with all the pictures of animals in it. I like the sounds you make. I like to feel the words and the colors. Please read the animal book again. I'm learning all the names of the animals and I like it when you ask me to tell you their names.

Language (BAD)

You say goddamit, Dad says son of a bitch. Can I say son of a bitch? What can I say when I get angry?

I am learning words. I have a whole bunch of new ones, *go out, want cookie, pick up, read book*. I like being able to tell you what I want. I am also learning some words that help me express my strong feelings. Mostly I learn my words from you. I hear how you use them and then I use them that way, too. Today I used the word *baby* for the first time when our friend Susan came over with her new baby. You smiled and let me hold the baby for a minute. I got a very different reaction when I used the word *goddamit* for the first time today. I heard you use it when you dropped the noodles in the sink. I dropped the blankets I was carrying, so I used it, too. I was mad and saying that made me feel better. Why did you say I shouldn't use that word again?

I'M CONFUSED. WHAT I NEED FOR YOU TO DO IS:

> Teach me that there are
> "good" and "bad" words.

W hy can't I say *goddamit*? Are there really some words that are bad? Why are they bad? How will I

86

know which ones are good and which ones are bad? It would help if we thought of some strong words that I could say that wouldn't upset anyone. I need to be able to express my strong feelings, too. And please don't yell at me if I use another "bad" word, just let me know it's ones of those "bad ones."

Let's work together to clean
up the "bad" language.

Why do you use bad words? You can help me use only good words if you used them, too. Since I'm learning my language from you I need your help here. Maybe you could use the same strong words that you suggested for me: "I'm mad" or "Darn it."

LISTENING

I am listening. I am listening to my favorite song on TV.

There are lots of good sounds in our house. When I hear the heater hum I know that warm air is coming out and I can go warm my toes. I hear the sounds from the airplanes that fly over our house, the water filling the bathtub, and the purring of the cat. I hear you hum quietly while you get breakfast ready. But sometimes when I'm busy watching TV or playing with my trucks I don't hear the cat, the heater, or your voice when you say it's time for breakfast.

YOU GET ANGRY WHEN I DON'T HEAR EVERY WORD YOU SAY. IT WOULD HELP IF YOU WOULD:

Make sure you have my attention.

You expect that I will hear you when you stand in the kitchen and yell across the room. If you really want me to hear you, you need to come over by me, sit next to me, and touch my hand gently. I hear you better when we are eye to eye. Then tell me "It's breakfast time and you need to come to the table as soon as this song is over." Turning off the TV when the song ends will help me remember what I'm suppose to be doing.

Tell me what to do and then help me do it.

No standing on the sofa. Stop playing with your straw! Don't splash in the bath. All day long you tell me what I'm not supposed to do. Sometimes I stop and sometimes I don't. Sometimes I am just checking to see how many times you will say no before you come and take me off the sofa. Why do you say the same thing over and over? If you really want me to stop, get my attention and tell me sofas are for sitting. Then come and sit by me and give me a hug and tell me I am being a good listener. When I play with my straw, remind me that straws are for drinking and that if I continue to play with it you will take it away. And at bath time show me how I can practice swimming without getting water all over the bathroom. Tell me what to do not just what not to do. Then I'll know what should happen.

Give me lots of positive messages.

Sometimes I know what you're going to say and I don't like it. When that happens I won't look you in the eyes, that way I won't hear you. JOHN, PICK UP YOUR CARS NOW! feels so bad. But I listen when you sit down next to me and tell me it's time to drive the cars into the garage. I also like it when you say things like "John, it's so nice to see you this morning," or "Wow, I saw you zoom down that slide" or "Thank you for helping me set the table." Please make sure that there are more good-feeling messages than nos.

LYING

I didn't spill the juice! No, I didn't!

Spilling juice is bad and I'm not bad. I try to do good things, it's just that sometimes bad things happen. I didn't mean to spill my juice. So I wish that I hadn't spilled the juice, that the juice just fell over on its own. I wished so hard that now I'm sure that the glass just tipped, that is what really happened. I'm a good girl, I wouldn't have spilled it.

I DON'T MEAN TO LIE. HERE'S HOW TO WORK WITH ME ON THIS:

> *Don't expect me to be perfect.*

It's so easy to make mistakes when you are two. I didn't know that when you put the cup on the edge of the place mat it would tip. Please don't yell at me, I just didn't know. I tell you I didn't do it so you won't be disappointed in me. Help me not to be scared when an accident happens. It would be good if you showed me that cups always have to be where it's flat or they are more likely to spill. I would like to help clean up the mess. Tell me that spills happen and whenever I spill something you would like to know right away, because it's easier to clean up right after it happens. Have you ever made a mistake? When you do, if you ever spill anything I would like it if you said, "Oh, Oh I made a mistake, time to clean it up." Can I help you clean?

Don't worry about my tall tales.

I have a dog named Sam. He can do tricks. I play ball with him and give him bones. There is an aligator named Katie who lives under my bed, she keeps me safe at night. I can see all kinds of fun things in my mind and I like to talk about them. Is there something wrong with that? Sometimes I get confused about what is real and what isn't. Other people get confused, too. I don't really understand what a lie is. Is it kind of like make-believe? Aaron wanted to come over and see my dog. You could tell him that my dog, Sam, is invisible and only I can see him.

These aren't lies, they are just my imagination exploring ideas and stories from my mind. They help me shape my world and are the way I would like things to be. My stories give me power and security.

Manners

I want cookie! I want cookie! Pleeease?

I am learning to using my words to tell you what I want. Using words is good, when I used my words to tell Miles I wanted the red truck he gave it to me. Before I would just grab the toy I wanted and sometimes the other kid wouldn't let go. At first I just said "cookie" to let you know I wanted a cookie. Now I can use three words to tell you what I want. What is the magic word? Why do I have to say "please" before you give me a cookie?

HERE'S HOW TO HELP ME LEARN MANNERS:

Tell me that words can be nice.

I need to know there are some special words I can use to make what I'm saying sound nice. You like it when I say "Cookie please." After I get the cookie, if I want to sound nice I can say "thank you." Using nice words makes other people feel good and feel better about me.

Use your best manners.

I feel better when people use these words, too. I like it when you say "please" and "thank you" to me. I don't always remember to say them, but when I hear you say them it helps me remember. If you expect me to use good manners use the right words and good manners yourself. This shows me how to speak and behave correctly. Today I heard you say "please" to my teacher, to my friend Whitney, and to our neighbor Shawn. When Grandma left you said, "Thank you for coming over." That must of made Grandma feel good because she got a big smile on her face. I am learning that lots of people like to hear "please" and "thank you."

Pleeease don't force my nice words.

It's not that I don't want to use "please" and "thank you," it's just that I forget. Don't you forget, it hasn't been all that long ago since I didn't have any words at all. Using words isn't always so easy. I get frustrated when you tell me I can't have a cookie until I say the magic word. I don't like it when you tell me what I have to say. What I like is when you notice my nice words and say "Matthew, you are doing such a good job of remembering to say 'please' and 'thank you.'" Those are nice words, too.

Masturbation

*When I rub my blanket between my legs
it feels so good.*

Since I started wearing big boy pants I've noticed that when I rub my penis gently I feel all good inside. It feels so good that I do it when I'm just sitting watching television, before I go to sleep, or whenever I just think of it. Most of the time you're busy and don't notice what I'm doing, but when you do you tell me to "stop that right now." You really don't want me to rub my penis, I can tell by the color of your face and the sound of your voice. I do other things that make my body feel good, like running fast, touching my arm with a feather, and stroking my face with my blanket and you don't get angry. What's the problem with my penis? If it bothers you, I will just wait until you're busy and not looking.

HERE 'S HOW TO WORK WITH ME ON THIS:

Teach me about privacy.

It's my body and I like making it feel good. You need to tell me that there are different rules for different activities. Running as fast as you can is fun, but it is best done outside, so things don't get knocked over and broken. Touching your penis feels good, but it is not good manners to do it in public. It is best done when you are alone, in private. So, if I want to rub myself I need to go to my room. I will need some help remembering about privacy, so please help me by saying (in your nice voice), "Matthew, it looks like you need a little privacy."

Mealtime

"Sit down." "Eat another bite of your broccoli." "Stop playing with your casserole." "Get back in your chair and finish your dinner."

Why do I have to stay at the table and eat? I have cars to drive into the garage and a fire truck that needs to put out a fire. I'm not hungry! Besides why should I eat this broccoli when I can get you to give me some crackers after dinner? And what do eating and sitting have to do with each other?

IF IT'S REALLY IMPORTANT TO YOU THAT I EAT DINNER WITH YOU THEN YOU SHOULD TRY THESE:

Make sure I'm hungry at dinnertime.

I get hungry before dinner is ready and you give me a snack. Then when it's time to eat dinner, I have problems, I haven't had time to get hungry. When I'm not hungry I just can't sit at the table. If you make me stay at the table I start to play with my food. I don't have anything else to do. Try giving me my snack earlier in the afternoon. That way when I get to the table I'll be hungry.

Don't talk to me about food.

Just give me my food and let me decide what and how much I will eat. I'm learning to listen to my body and to know when I am full. I will protest if you try to force me to eat more. I do not want to talk about my eating. I'm in charge of what goes in my mouth. Some days the potato tastes really good and I will eat lots and another time I'm just not so hungry. Don't put lots of food on my plate, I get overwhelmed. Let me ask for more of the things that taste good.

Make me wait until snack time.

I like snack food better than dinner foods. Crackers, cookies, banana, and cheese are my favorites. So I eat a little of my dinner, go to check on my fire truck, come back when you tell me to sit down, and then play with my casserole. Finally you say, "Josh, you must be done with dinner," and you let me get down from the table. That's okay because I know you will give me a snack as soon as I demand it.

You say we just had dinner, that I should eat a better dinner, and then you get me my snack. If you really want me to eat a better dinner include at least one food that you know I will like. Grownups eat really yucky foods. I don't like that stuff, I know, even though I haven't tried it. Let me know that I can decide when I am done with dinner, but that once I get down from the table dinner is over. There won't be any more food until snack time, and that won't be until after my bath.

Please make dinnertime pleasant.

I like to be with you. But at dinnertime you talk to each other and don't pay any attention to me. The TV is on and you pay attention to it and you keep getting up and down to answer the phone. If you want me to sit down, you sit down. Have the entire family sit down. I'd like to talk about the birds we saw outside today or the bubbles I played in at day care. If you want dinnertime to be a family time then you need to include me. It's nice when we are all together.

MEDICATIONS

If I don't like the taste of something you tell me that I don't have to eat it. I tried pickles, peaches, and yellow cheese and I didn't like them. I don't like the taste of medicine. Why do you force me to eat it?

You want me to take that white medicine. It smells and it tastes really bad. No! I won't. I will decide what I eat. I will clamp my mouth down. And if you somehow get some in my mouth I'll spit it up. Why does it taste so bad?

OUR FIGHTS OVER MEDICINE TAKE A LOT OF MY ENERGY, LET'S FIND A BETTER WAY.

Explore ways to make it taste better.

I'm already sick, the taste makes me feel more yucky. Don't tell me it tastes good, it doesn't. Instead tell me that you know that sometimes medicines don't taste so good. That you are going to try to find a way to make it taste better. Maybe the doctor or the person at the drugstore will have some ideas. They might know a medicine that tastes okay. Tell them that I have a mouth that likes to eat things that taste good. Things like ice cream, yogurt, and applesauce. Maybe the docter would say it was okay to have my medicine with yogurt.

I could try eating a Popsicle before I took my medicine. When your mouth is really cold your taster doesn't work as well. Or I could try holding my nose when I take the medicine, it's not supposed to taste so bad that way. I would probably need some juice to drink right after to get the taste out of my mouth. Even after the medicine is out of my mouth, my mouth still tastes yucky.

Tell me why I really need to take medicine.

If I understand why I need my medicine I might take it, but I'm not going to like it. I need to hear "Your throat hurts when you swallow. The medicine is going to help your throat get better." Even though I want to feel better I will fight you on the medicine. I have to find out if I really have to take it or if you will let me out of it if I put up a fuss. If I must take the medicine give me a choice of how to take it. Let's see, I think I'd like a blob of brown sugar and some orange seltzer water with my medicine today.

Naps

*It's nap time you say. I say no, I've got too
many things to do to stop now.*

The sun is shining and I love to be outside, where
I can dig in the sandbox, give my dolls a bath in
the wading pool, search for shiny rocks, and dig a
hole in the garden with my shovel. How about if
you just let me play. I don't feel tired. Maybe if I
do get tired I'll lay down on my own and go to
sleep. Not willing to take the chance? Why doesn't
sister take a nap? Why not you? I'm the only one
who has to take a nap. I think that you're the one
who really needs a nap. You sure are cranky sometimes. Remember those days when I just fell
asleep in your arms and you laid me in my crib,
that was so much easier.

You know if I don't take a nap then by dinnertime I am too tired and likely to have a meltdown
over anything that doesn't go my way. I don't
really like to be overtired, but at nap time I am not
easily convinced. You see I live in the moment, and
right this moment I need to fill this bucket full of
water from the pool and water those flowers over
there.

GETTING ME TO TAKE A BREAK IS IMPORTANT,
HERE ARE A FEW THINGS YOU CAN TRY.

Establish a regular rest time and routine.

I have trouble stopping in the middle of my play to go nap. If each day after snack time we go up to my room for a rest I would (after a period of testing) come to expect it. At day care we always lay down after snack time. Just like at bedtime I need a routine that tells my body it's time to relax and rest. We could read a story and then I could listen to some music.

Please avoid running errands before nap time. I often fall asleep in the car but sleep for only a short period. Catnaps make me feel good for a little while but don't give me enough energy to make it to bedtime. Being two takes a lot of energy . . . doesn't it?

Provide extra help when I'm overtired.

Yesterday we had such a busy morning, we went swimming and then had a picnic in the park. When I got home I started running all over the house, chasing the cat. I was overtired and really had a lot of trouble getting my body to settle down. That's why I started screaming and crying. I needed your help to get to sleep. When I am overtired back rubs sometimes help. What helps most is when you hold me, I love to snuggle with you.

It doesn't feel good to be overtired. I need breaks on really busy days for some quiet activities. Then I might not get overtired in the first place.

Enforce a rest time, but don't insist I sleep.

You can put me in my bed but you can't make me sleep. Today I am particularly stubborn. I am feeling a need to be in control. I don't want to be told what to do. Don't fight me on this, it won't be pretty and you can't win. What you can do is tell me that while I don't have to sleep I do have to stay quiet in my bed for one hour. Give me the choice of looking at some books or playing with a few plastic animals. Set the timer and leave. If I come out of my room, calmly remind me it is rest time and walk me back. I will probably make a fuss to make sure you really mean it. If I get used to this I might even take a nap.

Nightmares

It was chasing me, the dog with the big teeth, it was making a noise.

When I was a baby I was busy learning about things close to me—people, toys, pots and pans, shoes, nothing scary. But now I see things that I don't understand, like people getting hurt, monsters and animals with really big teeth. When I think about these things I get scared. Sometimes I see bad things in my sleep, and I start to cry. Then I see you and hear your voice, but I can still see that dog.

I NEED YOUR HELP GETTING BACK TO SLEEP. WHAT I NEED YOU TO DO IS:

Reassure me and stay with me.

Sometimes I wake up and then go right back to sleep. Other times I can't get the scary picture out of my mind and I can't get back to sleep. The bad things are gone but they feel like they are still here. Will they come back? I need you to hold me, protect me, I get so scared. Please don't put me back in my bed and leave, I'm little and I can't protect myself. I need to hear "You had a bad dream, I'm here and you are safe." Rock me and sing me my favorite song. That helps me feel better. When I feel safe I can go back to sleep.

Make nighttime peaceful.

I'm more likely to have a nightmare on a night when I watch TV before bed or when Dad tickles me right before bed. I guess I get a little too excited. Maybe TV and tickling should be earlier in the day and right before bed we should read and listen to music. It's easier to go to sleep when we've had some quiet time together.

No!

*"It's time for breakfast." "No!" "Would you
like to look at books?" "No!" "It's bath
time, okay?" "No!" "Do you want to wear
your bug shirt or your cowboy shirt?"
"No!" "It's time to get in the car."
"No, No, No!"*

It has been a busy and tiring morning. You wish I
would just do what you ask me to do. But I can't. I
am learning to think and act for myself. You're always running everything. *No* gives me a chance to
be in charge. I am not you and I need to decide
what I like and what I want. Sometimes I'm not
sure what I want, so when you give me a choice I
say no. I need to feel in control. That's hard to do,
when you're always told what to do and what not
to do. It's really hard to feel in control when we
run errands and I keep having to get in and out of
the car seat, we go in and out of stores, and I never
get to look at or touch anything. When I'm really
feeling a need for control I'll even say no if you ask
if I want an ice-cream cone (I love ice cream). Then
I will cry because I didn't get any.

I AM TRYING TO BE MORE INDEPENDENT. HERE'S HOW YOU CAN HELP:

Allow me a few hundred nos a day.

I am only doing what every two-year-old must do. Don't get angry at me, learning how to be independent is hard work. No, I do not want to eat my cracker at the table or the counter. I want to eat it right here, on the floor in front of the refrigerator. When you calmly listen to my ideas and let me have my way, it makes me feel good. By telling me that what's important to you is that where I eat is easy to clean up, I also learn why you said yes.

Sometimes I need time to make a decision. Don't take my quick no as my final word. By asking me to name my favorite ice cream you help me get unstuck from no and to start thinking about how much I really do want ice cream.

Don't worry, allowing me to think for myself and have my way sometimes will not turn me into a spoiled monster. If I am allowed to say no now, it will be easier to say when I get older. You don't want me to say yes to everything, do you?

Make your requests clear.

Sometimes I get very confused. You say "It's time for bath, okay?" I say no. You did ask if it was okay.

Well it's not okay, I'm busy. If you really want me to go up for my bath you first need to warn me. Say something like "bath in five minutes." I hate surprises. Then give me a choice. "Would you like to hop like a bunny up to your bath or fly like a bird?" I think tonight I will roar like a tiger on the way to the bath.

Use fewer nos yourself.

I hear no from you all day long. "No, you can't wear Mommy's ring. No, you can't grab the dog's tail. No, you can't have a cookie." It gets very frustrating. Does that ever happen to you? I feel much better when you show me and tell me what I can do. Oh, I can't wear Mommy's ring but I can dance with Mommy's scarf. Thanks!

Nudity

I like being naked.

I'm learning how to dress and undress myself. I particularly like to practice the undressing part. Once I've taken all my clothes off, I like to run around the house, and when it's warm I like to be outside. The sun feels good on my body. Sometimes you just smile and say, "There's Monica in her birthday suit again." But sometimes you say I'm bad and grab me and pull my clothes back on me. I scream and hit and kick when you do that. Stop doing that to me, I was having so much fun. Why do I have to wear clothes?

I'M CONFUSED. WHAT I NEED FOR YOU TO DO IS:

Tell me why I need to wear clothes.

You could say birds have feathers, cats have fur, but we have skin. Clothing is like our fur or our feathers. Without it our skin sticks to the car seat, we get ouchies when we fall down, and we can get really cold. In the summer we wear clothes that help us stay cool and in the winter we wear warm clothes to keep us feeling toasty.

Tell me about manners.

Why is it all right for me to be naked sometimes and not others? I need to know that bodies are private and that people wear clothes when they go outside their homes and when they have guests. So I am to keep my clothes on when I go to my friend Sara's house and when Grandmom and Grandpa come over to our house. That is using good manners. But I can run naked for a few minutes after my bath before it is time to get my nightclothes on.

Parent Disagreements

"Daddy, kiss Mommy. Mommy talk to Daddy, please."

Please stop, be nice, use your inside voices. I like it when you are paying attention to me and we are laughing and smiling. How can I get you to smile again?

I GET SCARED WHEN YOU YELL AT EACH OTHER. HERE'S WHAT I NEED YOU TO DO:

Assure me I will be okay.

When you use your loud voice at me, I get all upset inside. When you two use them at each other I don't know what to do. It makes me feel really bad and the bad feelings don't go away. This is the most frightening situation for me. The people I depend on to keep my world are out of control. I need you to say "Josh, Mommy and Daddy are angry because we have different ideas. That happens sometimes. We are okay and we both love you. We are going to try to find a good solution to our problem."

114

Remember I am learning from you.

If you throw things, slam doors, and hit each other when you are angry I will learn that is how grown-ups handle their disagreements. You tell me not to scream and say bad things. Why do you? Anger makes people do scary things. Are there less scary ways to be angry? Can people still love each other after they're angry? I need reassurance that even though you don't always think the same way, you can still love each other. I have so many questions but I don't have the words.

PARENT PREFERENCE

When Mommy tucks me in bed she goes
Hummm and gives me a big hug. Then I call
her a noisy hugger and we laugh. Go away!
I want Mommy to put me to bed, not you!

My mommy is so special. She's been taking care of me forever. She and I have ways of doing things. We bop down the stairs after teeth brushing, and she opens the juice and then lets me pour it into my cup and when I get an ouchie, she gives it a special kiss. I know my mommy and it feels so good and safe to be with her. Becoming a big kid can be hard sometimes. On those days when nothing is going right, I want my mommy!

I LIKE YOU TOO, DADDY, IT'S JUST THAT I DON'T
KNOW YOU AS WELL. HERE'S WHAT YOU MIGHT
DO:

Help Mom take care of me.

When I ask for some juice or a snack Mom is almost always the one who gets it. You don't seem to hear me, and when you do you have to ask Mom where the cups and lids are. It's easier to just have

Mom do it, she knows what she's doing. Maybe if you tried to take care of me more often I would learn that you can be as good as Mom.

Please don't get mad if I make a fuss when you are trying to get me ready for bed. Tell me "I know you would rather have Mom do this, she's the best Mom ever, but she can't do it right now." Be sure and let me know that she will be in soon for kisses and hugs.

Make some special time for me.

Maybe you could think of some fun thing we could do together, something Mommy doesn't do. I could help you wash the car or maybe you could show me your tools. I might even go with you to run an errand to the hardware store. But if you ask me if I want to go I'll probably say no, so it would be better if you told me that we were going to the hardware store in five minutes and that I was going to help you pick out the nails.

Mom is always around, but what if she went out to a movie without us? I would probably scream for a while. But after I calmed down, you and I could figure out how to get things done together. We can come up with our own special ways of doing things. Then I would start to look forward to my Dad nights.

PHONE CALLS INTERRUPTED

We were having so much fun giving my baby a bath until that phone rang. Stop talking on that phone!

When the phone rings you stop playing with me and give all of your attention to that phone. Getting my baby bathed, dried, and dressed is more important than any phone call. And I don't like it when you're on the phone when I'm eating or watching a video. I get scared, you're here but not paying any attention to me. So, I'll splash the water, ask for some juice, and pull the dog's tail to get you back with me. I want you to like me more than the phone.

I WANT YOUR ATTENTION. HERE ARE A FEW WAYS WE CAN AVOID PHONE HASSLES:

Get a machine to answer the phone.

At Micah's house they have a machine that answers their phone. His mom lets us listen to her voice on the machine and we listened to the voices of other people. That was really neat. Sometimes there wasn't a message only a click sound, I guess that person didn't want to leave a message. If we got one of those machines we wouldn't have to stop playing to answer the phone.

Avoid long phone calls and stay close.

If you really need to talk into that phone, please don't do it for very long. I'm not very patient and I'm not old enough to understand that some calls may be necessary or important. Those are things I can learn maybe when I'm three. Maybe if you stayed by me and helped me dry my doll while you were talking, that would be okay. Most of the time you walk away from me when you're talking on the phone. Micah's mom has a phone with no string. She can be where we are. Could we get one of those?

And I'd like to try talking into the phone, too. But it's kind of scary. Maybe I should try talking into my toy phone. I would like it if you called me on my phone, that would be fun. Or we could pretend to call Grandma.

PLAY WITH ME!

Hooray! You're finally sitting down. I've watched you put the groceries away, start the washing machine, and take the dog out to go potty. Now I want some of your attention. I want you to play with me!

I like to play with you. When we play with the blocks you show me new ways to stack them. We build big houses together. You push me really fast in my car. I like that. When I'm building a fort with the sofa cushions you help me find a way to keep them from falling down. Then you help me gather all my dolls and blankets to put in the fort. I learn a lot when I play with you. You give me ideas, help me solve problems, and teach me words that help me to understand and to expand what I am doing. You always share and do what I want to do. Sometimes when I play with children they hit me and take my toys. You are the perfect playmate.

The best is when you don't do anything else— just sit with me and play. Those are my favorite times. A lot of times I want to play with you and you say no, you have something else you need to do. Wait! I need you. I don't care that you would like time to yourself. I need to play, and you're the only one who lets me be in charge.

HERE'S HOW TO WORK WITH ME ON THIS:

Play with me first.

I need time with you every day. I will interrupt, cling, and whine until you play with me. It would

save me a lot of energy if you would start the day playing with me. Once we've spent some time together then I'm ready to go off on my own to explore some new ideas. When I get home from day care at night I like it best when we sit and read a story. After we've had some time to snuggle, then I can play by myself while you go change your clothes.

Get me started and then stay nearby.

I like it when you get out the paints or the Play-Doh before dinner. Then I can sit at the counter and play and still have you near me if I need some help or want to show you what I have done. When you have things you need to do I can help. I like to wipe the cleaner off the mirror, empty the waste-basket, and wash the dishes in really bubbly water.

I get scared when you say you need a time-out. Bad children get time-outs. Did you do something bad? I need you. When will you be my mommy again? It would help me if you set the timer and tell me that you are going to read your magazine for fifteen minutes and that I can sit next to you and look at my books or I can color. Tell me that you need a little quiet time. I think I can do that.

POTTY (REFUSING TO USE)

No! I don't want to sit on the potty and you can't make me.

Right when I was in the middle of building a hill in the sand you make me stop to go sit on the potty. I'm too busy to sit on the potty. You like the potty, I am not interested in the potty. I will decide when I am ready. The more you push the potty the more I will refuse.

You say I am growing so big that it's time to use the potty like the big boys. But I'm not so sure I want to be a big boy. I'm not tall enough to use the potty like a big boy. I don't know if I can do it, and besides I like being a baby. Does being a big boy mean that you won't carry me or rock with me anymore?

I know you don't like changing my diaper, I can tell by the way you scrunch up your nose when you change me. I've been wearing them for two years now, and I'm used to them.

*WHAT I NEED FROM YOU MOST IS PATIENCE. WAYS
YOU CAN WORK WITH ME ON THIS INCLUDE:*

Wait until I'm ready to begin
toilet training.

Right now I am not interested in using the potty. Someday, probably soon, I'll be more aware of when I pee or poop in my diaper. I will prefer being clean and will want you to change me right away. Then you can tell me that if I use the potty I won't have the yucky feeling from a wet diaper. My friends are starting to use the potty and I will watch them and see what they do.

Let me be in control. Teach me things I need to know but let me make the decisions about my body. Help me recognize when I need to go by telling me that when I cross my legs you can see I need to go potty. Show me that it's easier to get sweatpants and shorts off when I need to go and that my favorite snap front jeans are just too hard to get off. Let me decide if I am going to wear a diaper or underpants each day. I like my new Batman underpants, but on some days I may feel a little unsure about making it to the potty. And I don't want to pee on Batman.

POWER STRUGGLES

When I was a baby you made the decisions. But now that I am two I am learning to think for myself. I have my own ideas about how I want to spend my time, what I want to wear, and what tastes good to me.

You think I am too young to make decisions or have ideas. I have lots of ideas, so do you. Unfortunately you and I often don't have the same ideas. Today I wanted to jump on the sofa, wear all my necklaces to the grocery store, walk without holding your hand in the parking lot, and have a Popsicle with lunch. These things are so important to me that I continue to ask even after you have said no. You are bigger than me so you get your way. But I scream and kick in protest. Why do you always have to have your way? Do you get angry when other people have ideas that are different from yours? Or is it just me? Why won't you listen and try my way sometimes? When I hear no all day long I feel helpless. You make the choices because it is easier for you. Easy isn't always best. Don't you want me to learn to be independent?

INSTEAD OF FIGHTING WITH ME I WISH YOU WOULD:

Find ways to say yes.

You say no to my ideas so quickly. Do you really think about what I'm asking? What would be the worst thing that would happen if I wore my necklaces to the grocery store? Why is what I wear so important to you? I would like you to tell me that you can see that today I am a girl who wants to wear her jewels. When you say yes to my ideas it makes me feel so good.

I climb, run, and jump all around the house because I am learning to move my body. I need a space to play that says yes. Our house is filled with nos. Don't jump on the sofa, don't climb on the table, and don't run in the hall. But I want to jump, I need to jump, if I can't jump on the sofa where can I jump? I can handle "no jumping on the sofa" if you tell me that I can jump, on the little trampoline or on the bed in my room. Give me toys that let me use my body—a rocking horse, a slide, and a large ball to bounce on. Give me some space, clear away things that I might break and let me move.

Avoid saying no.

It's very tiring and frustrating to fight all day long. When I hear a lot of nos from you I continue to push. I'm trying to have some power. You say no all the time. I can say no, too. All of your requests will be met with a loud no! I'm more likely to be cooperative if you say "Let's find your teddy and get him ready for his nap" than if you say "Are you ready for nap?" or "It's time for nap, okay?"

Every day before dinner we put away the toys. I like knowing what will happen next, it makes me feel secure. We never fight over picking up toys. We do it together. You always let me choose what you're going to put away. I like that.

Choose your battles wisely.

Even though I want control over everything, I'm not ready to make every decision. When you say no to everything, no doesn't mean much anymore. Struggle with me about important issues like taking medicine and sitting in my car seat. I need you to protect me. I will learn (in time) that there are some issues that are not negotiable. Stop me when I climb on an unstable ladder and then remove it from my play space. But please don't fight with me over my choice of clothing colors and my desire to eat baked potatoes every night for dinner or my insistence that foods not touch one another on my plate. I need to feel in control of my life sometimes, don't you? I'm only two but I'm growing up.

PRETEND

"No! No jumping on the bed. Molly could get hurt! Ah, oh, Molly fell off. Mommy will kiss it and make it all better."

I like playing with my doll, Molly. She does many of the same things I do, she sits on the potty, takes a bath, and sleeps in a big bed. Sometimes she gets sick and has to go to the doctor. I tell her not to be scared, the doctor won't hurt her. I show her what the doctor will do, and that makes her feel better. Then I help her take her medicine.

I spend most of the day taking care of Molly. She needs me and I need her. I feel very grown-up and in control when I help her go to the potty and take a bath. When I comfort Molly before she goes to the doctor it helps me understand my own experiences at the doctor's office, and that makes me feel better. Sometimes she does things she's not supposed to do and I have to tell her no. But then I give her a big hug to let her know I still love her.

THERE IS SO MUCH TO UNDERSTAND WHEN YOU ARE TWO, AND PRETENDING HELPS. YOU CAN AID MY PRETENDING BY:

Giving me space and props.

I love it when you put a blanket over the table, then I have my very own house. It's my place, I'm in charge. Inside my house I make a place where Molly and I can have a snack. Then we look at books and visit with MooMoo, my cow. If Molly starts to feel sick I can get out my doctor's kit and make her feel better. I can be a doctor, now that Uncle Bill gave me a doctor's bag. With your shoes and blouse I can be a mother, with my cowboy hat on I can be a cowgirl, and with my crown on I am a princess. It's so much fun to pretend.

Remember this is my fantasy.

MooMoo is a flying cow and Molly is taking a ride, whee. You say cows don't really fly. But, this is my story, and in my story cows fly. I'm busy with my game, please don't interrupt. If I want you to see me I might fly by on my cow. Then ask me if you can feed the cow a little grass. He might be hungry, from all that flying. I might be hungry, too.

Regression

*Mommy, will you rock with me in the
rocking chair? Will you hold me like you
used to when I was a baby? I'm your baby.*

Preschool is fun. I get to paint, ride the rocking horse, and play in the bubbles. At snack time I put the napkins and the crackers on the table. The teacher said "Wow! What a big girl you are." Daddy, up. I want you to carry me to the car. I want to listen to my Jennifer tape, the one that has my name. When I get home I want my bottle, I don't want a cup today, I want a bottle. I want my blanket, even my big bed feels too big. Just hold me, please.

Please don't tell me to stop acting like a baby. The more you tell me to grow up the more I need the safety of being a baby. It's scary being a big girl. I am learning and trying so many new things. Much of the time I want to do it myself, and I scream if you do things for me. But it's so frustrating when I can't get my coat on or undo the snap on my pants.

IT'S HARD BEING A BIG GIRL. WAYS YOU CAN
SUPPORT ME INCLUDE:

Reducing the pressure.

People don't have so many things they want you to do when you're a baby. Babies don't have to use the potty, put on their own socks, drink from a cup, and sleep in a big bed. It takes a lot of energy to learn so many new things. I don't want to disappoint you or make you mad and I would like to get a sticker for using the potty, I just don't have the energy right now. I need fewer outings and more rest. When you let me be a baby again I feel safe and warm. I am only two.

Give me love, love, and more love.

Let's look at the pictures of when I was a baby. I love it when you tell me how happy you were when I was born, how much you loved me when I was a baby and how much you love me now. Tell me that you know how nice it is to be little and point out that there are some good things about being big, too. But don't talk about it too much. I'm trying to rest and feel secure. I'm changing very quickly, just give me a little time and lots of loving and patience and I will be off and running and jumping again.

Routines

No! My shirt first then pants, teeth brushing then hair brushing. We have a getting-ready routine and I insist you follow it.

In the morning you always say, good morning, good morning, good morning in your very friendly voice. Then you sit on the bed while I slowly open my eyes and stretch. Then we hug. It makes me feel so good. It's one of the best parts of the day. So many things frustrate and confuse me. This morning the dinosaur puzzle won't fit together and you said I couldn't wear my superhero shirt, that it is dirty. I don't care about dirt. Then it was breakfast time. You always let me choose between two breakfast cereals and two spoons. Knowing what is going to happen next and getting to choose helps me feel secure and in control. There are other things that we do that I look forward to during the day. At day care we always hang up my coat and my bag on my hook. You always give me two big kisses and two big hugs because I am two and then say "See you later alligator." When we get home you always sit in the rocking chair and talk for a few minutes, and then you go up and change your clothes. And at bedtime we always read two stories.

You get frustrated when I insist that we do it the right way. You think that I'm just being bossy, but I'm not. These routines are very important to me, and when we don't follow them or hurry too much I have real trouble.

HERE'S HOW TO WORK WITH ME ON THIS:

Stick to the routine.

Routines work for me. When I know that I will get to have special time with you in the morning, when you get home, and at bedtime then I don't have to work to get your attention at other times. Before we had a special good-bye, I got scared when you left me at day care. Now I can let you go and know that you will be back. When you say it is late and we don't have time for stories I get upset and have trouble getting to sleep. If we really don't have time for two stories, maybe we could read one really short one. Or we could pick a story to read tomorrow and set it by the bed. Be sure and tell me that tomorrow I will get my two bedtime stories, and then make sure I do.

*Provide lots of patience and familiar things
when my routine is disrupted.*

Change is hard. It is even harger when you don't plan for it. When we go to spend the night at Grandma's, try to make my daily schedule as normal as possible. With your support I can handle some change, but it will take a lot of my energy and a lot of yours too. Be sure and pack my books, my bubble bath and towel, and give me my special greeting every morning.

Safety

Ouchie, Mommy. I just wanted to cut my apple like you do. I didn't know that the knife would cut me, too!

I watch how you do things and I want to do it, too. I pick up the phone and push all the buttons like you do, I dig holes in the ground and plant flowers with you, and when you leave the room while cleaning the toilet I make the water blue just like you. I am eager to learn all about the things around me, so I spend my days tasting and touching everything within my reach. When I was a baby you put a gate on the stairs, moved the plants up where I couldn't reach them, and put locks on the drawers. I needed you to protect me from ouchies. Now that I can run, jump, and climb I really need you to protect me from me. I don't know what is dangerous. I just want to do everything.

I DON'T LIKE TO GET HURT. HERE ARE SOME WAYS YOU CAN KEEP ME SAFE:

Lock up items that can hurt me.

Please, please, please put away all the things that can hurt me. If you don't lock something up or put it away then it must be safe for me to be curious about it. I just don't have enough experience to know which things are dangerous and which aren't. You say, "Bryan, I told you never to pick up my lighter." The problem is I see things that are interesting and I want to know about them. I am so curious I don't remember that you said this was a no-no. Maybe when I'm three I'll have a better memory.

Talk to me about danger.

Now that I can climb I can reach most everything. I have found that I can pull my step stool from the bathroom or a chair over to get on the counter. I can even get the neat things on top of the refrigerator. When you see me, you yell no and come and take me down. Maybe instead of "no" you could say "danger." I hear "no" all day long—"No, don't splash the water" and "No, you can not have a cookie." You need to use something other than "no" to really get my attention. Teach me that some things are "hot" or "sharp," and that I am not to touch, that it could give me an ouchie. When you use a knife tell me, "This is not a toy. Daddy uses it very carefully so he doesn't hurt himself. It is only for grown-ups to use." When I climb on the counter, tell me "danger." Then take me down and tell me that I could fall and get an ouchie when I climb there. Then show me where I can climb safely.

If I refuse to hold your hand in the parking lot, tell me that people in cars can't always see children, so I must always hold a grown-up's hand. I can hold your hand or be carried. Tell me that I am very important to you and that you would never want anything to happen to me. Tell me that grown-ups need to be safe, too. Show me how you stop, look, and listen before crossing the street and how you use a car seat belt, too.

Keep a close eye on me.

Even with all your safety proofing, I seem to be able to get into things that hurt me. It would be best if you didn't leave me alone, even for a short time. I am really fast now and I can get into trouble before you or I know it, and I don't even know it is trouble.

Be prepared to care for my ouchies.

If I do get hurt, really, really hurt, I will need you to know what to do. Show me that if I ever have an ouchie that we have a first aid kit and that you have all the important phone numbers to call right by the phone. Let's play doctor, okay? I'll pretend I have an ouchie and you make it all better. Show me how you care for your ouchies. I learn almost everything from you.

SEXUAL CURIOSITY

*I love to be all naked and look at myself
in the mirror—I can get a better
look that way.*

I am an explorer. I want to learn about everything. When I was interested in sand all I wanted to do was spend time in my sandbox digging, dumping, and mixing sand. Now I am interested in bodies. My body is particularly interesting. I explore my body by poking it with my finger, tickling it, and rubbing it with my blanket. I like to listen to my heartbeat, blow air on the mirror after my bath, and watch the poop come out of my bottom. I'm also interested in other people's bodies. That's why I come running into your bathroom when I hear the shower running. I'm just noticing that not everyone's body is the same.

THERE IS SO MUCH TO LEARN ABOUT BODIES.
I'M GOING TO NEED YOUR HELP TO FIGURE
THIS ALL OUT.

Give me the real names for all of my
body parts. I can handle it.

I love to learn new words and really like it when we play "Where is your nose? Where is your belly button?" I am learning that my body has lots of parts, and now that I'm learning to use the potty I have found even more of my body. What is the name of the place where the poop comes out? Where does the pee come out, and what is the name of this little bump? When I ask you questions about "down there" you get kind of red in the face and start talking about something else. Don't you know the names? Or are you afraid the words are too hard for me? Remember I can learn really hard names like stegosaurus, tyrannosaurus rex, and triceratops. I'm sure I can learn these, too. I want to know!

Help me understand how people's bodies are different.

When I was at my friend Sam's house we went to the potty. He stands up when he pees, and the pee comes out his penis. Sam told me that is what it is called. Do you have a penis? How come girls are girls? I am very concerned about this. I need to know that boys, and girls, have some body parts that are different. Maybe we could go to the library and get a book with pictures of boys' and girl's bodies. When you just tell me things I sometimes have a hard time understanding, but when I see pictures then I understand better. Don't be surprised if I start looking more closely at my dolls, stuffed animals, and my cat. I want to see if they have the special boy and girl parts. It may seem that I am stuck on this but don't worry. After I have answered all of my questions about body parts (with your help) I will move on to something else.

Sharing

Taking one of my toys is like taking a part of me and I just can't allow that.

For my birthday Uncle Bill gave me a dump truck, Tommy gave me a fire truck, and Grandma gave me a book that shows all kinds of trucks. Everyone gave me toys that they especially picked for me. They know I am a boy who loves trucks. I very carefully line my trucks up and get very upset when Michael gets anywhere close to them. First I shout no, then I use my hands to push him away and say "mine." When he won't stay away I hit him. These are my toys. I don't want anyone to touch them.

Now that I am two I am putting a lot of energy into declaring myself as an independent person, separate from you and everyone else. My special possessions help me define who I am. Everything I want, I see as mine. You see I am just starting to understand the idea of ownership. So I grab and declare as mine Michael's tape player, toys at day care I was thinking about playing with, and the slide at the park.

My possessiveness makes it hard for me to play with other kids at times. Only after I have had a chance to explore being a separate person, and have my own things, can I share.

HERE ARE SOME IDEAS FOR HELPING THE DAYS GO SMOOTHER.

Don't expect me to share.

Don't force me to share my toys with Michael. I get really angry when you set the buzzer and make me give my dump truck to Michael for a turn when it rings. I was playing and I wasn't done. I'm not sure when you force me to give my truck to Michael that it is still mine. It sounds better when you say "I see you are busy playing with your trucks. Michael would like to play with a truck, could you give him a turn when you are finished." And please could I have my own toy box, I don't want my toys in with Michael's.

When a friend comes over like Tommy, it helps if he brings some of his toys. Then we can each play with our own toys or maybe Tommy might let me play with his police car and I might let him play with my fire truck. This doesn't always happen easily and we might need your help to make it happen.

If Tommy and I are really fighting over who is going to play with my fire truck, please put it up. Then take us outside where we can run and explore. Sharing seems to be an inside-the-house problem.

Let's put my special things away before a friend comes over.

Things that are new are particularly hard for me to share, so let's put those toys away before a friend comes over. You don't share all of your things (the car, favorite sweater, special vase) with your friends, do you? You could ask me "What things would you like to put away before Tommy comes over?" and "What things should we set out for you two to play with?" Tommy and I rarely fight over Play-Doh, stickers, crayons, and blocks. There's a lot of those.

Show me how to share.

I need to learn about sharing, and I can do that by watching you share. I see you share the wheelbarrow with our neighbor Dan. When it snowed he gave us his shovel and we gave it back when the driveway was cleared off. Our neighbor Joyce always shares her cookies, she's my favorite.

I am starting to get the idea that sharing can feel good. Yesterday you told me, "Look how happy Tommy is that you shared your truck with him."

SHYNESS

*"I'm sorry, Mommy, I just want to stay
with you. I don't want to play."*

I like it when a friend comes over to my house. I particularly like it when my friend JoAnn comes over. We put on dress-up clothes, run around the house, and laugh in the mirror. Then we take those clothes off and try on some more. It's so fun. I don't play so well when we go to play group. You take me into the room with lots of other children and tell me to play. Then you start talking to another Mommy. I don't know this place, I feel alone, don't leave me, I don't know what to do. Your leg is a safe place, so I wrap my arms around it.

Play group day is hard on both of us. You get frustrated with me and I feel bad that I made you sad. You feel like quitting the group, that it's not worth the hassle. But please don't quit, I need to learn about people and things.

You wish I would go play like the other children and wonder why I stay stuck to you. Well, each time we go to play group we visit a different house. There are so many new things, more than I can handle at first. I am only two remember and there's a lot I don't understand. You may not now appreciate my need to feel in control before entering a new situation, but just wait until I'm a teenager, you'll be glad that I don't just jump in with the other kids.

HERE'S HOW YOU CAN HELP ME:

Give me time to warm up.

Next Tuesday before we go to play group take a minute to tell me where we are going and who will be there. Let's get there a little early before everyone else comes when it's quiet. Walk with me around the room and talk to me about the toys. I'm sure I'll find something that looks neat to play with. Sit down with me while I get started playing and stay there until I move away from you. I will need to be able to see you at all times. I never know what will happen, and I might need you. Sometimes when I get scared just seeing you helps, but at other times I will scream and need you right away. It may be many play group days before I move out on my own, but each time I learn more about how all this works and one day I will let go of your leg.

Don't call me shy.

I don't like the word *shy*. I'm not sure I know what it means. It doesn't sound good and I am good.

Help me to understand how I am feeling by saying "Sometimes when you are in a new place you need some time to check it out. I will stay with you until you are ready to explore on your own."

Help other people understand that I am a good thinker and that I take my time. Tell them that by watching I am learning about how each house is different and how children play. I'm not shy when I'm at home or at Grandma's house.

Help me have positive experiences.

I feel the best when I am with my things, I know all about them. I like playing best with just one friend, more than that is just, well, too much. But new places can be kind of neat, too. I got to play the piano at Sara's house, and at Peter's house I got to pet the kitty. I'd like to go back to those houses, I'd like to do that again. Invite them to our house, I feel really good here. But hide some of my toys, so they can't get hurt.

SIBLING (BABY)

*You're not my mommy anymore, now
you're Brendan's mommy. Take that baby
back! I want my mommy back!*

You said being a big brother would be great. You were wrong. Being a big brother is bad, nothing is the same, I don't like it. How would you feel if Daddy brought home a new wife and you had to share him? Before the baby came, I had you all to myself. When I asked for a cracker you got it. We would read two stories every night at bedtime, and when I was playing with my cars I could look at you and you would smile back. Now when I want a cracker you tell me I'll have to wait, you are feeding the baby. When we start to read, the baby begins to cry and you leave me, then Dad turns the lights off and says good night. No! I'm not ready for bed, I need my books. And I don't get any smiles because you are only smiling at the baby. What's so good about babies anyway? If you really liked me why did you get another baby?

*WHAT'S SO GOOD ABOUT BEING A BIG BROTHER?
HERE ARE SOME WAYS YOU CAN HELP ME WITH
THIS:*

Let me pretend to be a baby.

Mommy, I want a bottle! No, that is my rattle! I'm the baby! When the baby cries you jump up

and pick him up. He gets whatever he needs. But I am told to wait, or go find something to play with, you used to play with me. Maybe if I was a baby instead of a two-year-old you would spend your time with me. There are a lot of good things about being a baby, being rocked, sung to, cuddling with my blanket and pacifier. So when I act like a baby it is because I want you to love me and care for me as much as you do the baby.

Please don't tell me to stop acting like a baby. It scares me. I'm afraid you won't love me anymore. Let me be your baby, too. Hold me, and give me a bottle if I insist. Assure me I will always be your baby even when I'm a grown-up. Tell me the story about the day I was born and how glad you were to have me in your family.

Help me feel loved as a big boy. I like it when we look at my pictures when I was a baby and now that I'm a big boy. You always tell me you loved me then and you love me now. I need to hear that a lot right now. I'm not sure you can love both me and the baby. Let's make a list of all the things that the baby can't do. He can't eat an ice-cream cone, go down the slide, or even ride a trike. Then we can make a list of all the things that I can do. Tell me that I don't have to act like a baby to get cuddled and be loved. If I need to cuddle I can say "Cuddle, Mommy." Hey, being a big boy is pretty good. With all the focus on the baby I forgot. Once I start to feel good about being two again I won't be interested in doing baby things anymore. But please don't expect too much of me, having to share you with him is really hard. I was born first, does that mean I am still first?

Try to maintain my routines.

You used to say good morning, good morning, good morning to me with a big smile when you first came in the room. We used to snuggle on the sofa and watch my favorite TV show every morning. And you used to always brush my teeth and read to me. Now I watch TV alone, get up by myself, and hardly ever get to read books. So much is changing, it's scary. Why can't some things be the same?

Tell the baby you are going to have some special time with me.

My parents are the most important people in my world. Since the baby came here I have gotten to spend more time with Dad. That's been nice. I really liked going to the creek with him and pretending we were fishing. But I really miss you, Mommy. You were the best mommy ever, my mommy. You use to push me in my swing, talk with me while I drove cars, and dig with me in the garden. We don't do any fun things together anymore. Maybe Daddy could take care of the baby while you and I had some special time together. That would make me feel really good.

Let me help care for the baby.

I am kind of interested in the baby. He has such little hands. I handed him a toy, but he didn't even want it. He didn't take it, anyway. I am a big boy and there are a lot of ways big boys can help. I could help you change him by handing you a wipe, and then a diaper. I could color a picture for the baby's room and I could hold the baby. Show me how I can make him smile and ask me what I think he wants when he is crying. That way I will start to think of him as a person (not just a dumb baby) who has needs, too.

Be sure not to leave me by myself with the baby. I don't know much about babies and I might hurt him by accident. Sometimes I love him a little too hard. And I might hit him, some days it's hard to be a big brother. At those times when I'm feeling so frustrated or angry that I try to hurt him, say to me "I know that you're angry at the baby, but I'm not going to let you hurt him." Give me a hug and tell me you understand that having a new baby has been a big change for all of us and that change can be hard sometime.

Oh, and please don't give my special things to the baby. Even though I haven't used that key rattle in a long time it's still mine. Giving my things is like giving a part of me. I would like it if you would ask me what toys I would like to loan the baby. I think I might be able to do that, loan a few to him. Please don't get any more new babies.

SIBLING (CRAWLING)

You used to play with me, then we got a baby. He cried, and everyone spent time with him and I had to play alone. Now he is crawling and messing up my toys.

I had my animals all lined up and then Ryan crawled over and knocked them over. I screamed "Don't!" and hit him. He makes me so angry. He crawls right over to me and grabs my shirt then he pulls on my hair. Get away from me! Then he picked up my favorite truck, I grabbed it out of his hands. He started to cry. He has my crib, my car seat, and my clothes. I am not going to let him have my toys. Why do you yell at me whenever he cries? I am not a bad boy. It's his fault. Am I just supposed to let him knock over my toys and take my things?

I DON'T LIKE BABIES. HERE'S HOW YOU CAN HELP:

Don't expect me to share my toys.

I am only two. I am supposed to be exploring and exerting my independence. I am not ready to share my toys, and I don't have the language, self-control, or social skills to play with a baby. You tell me that the baby doesn't know that the truck is mine, to just let him have it. No! It's mine! How do I protect the things that are mine? You tell me what not to do—don't hit the baby, don't grab toys from Ryan. So what can I do? I need your help. Please don't leave me in a room alone with the baby. If you can't be in here with us he is likely to get hurt. He won't leave me alone, but I am stronger than he is.

Let's put Ryan's toys in one box and mine in another. I could even have two boxes. One box for toys I could loan to Ryan for a few minutes, I might even teach him how some of my toys work. In my other box I could put all my most special things that I don't have to share. We could put my special box where Ryan can't reach it and I could get it out when he is taking a nap.

Please think about my side.

It seems like I am always getting in trouble since that baby came. I need you to tell me that you understand how hard it is when Ryan takes one of my toys or messes up my things. Tell me that you do not want me to grab toys from Ryan, and that I am not allowed to hit, but that if I need something to come and get you. Show me how I can get my toy back by offering Ryan something else to play with. Then I won't have to come get you as often. Having this baby in my space gets in the way of my exploration. Please sometimes just let me play by myself.

SIBLING FIGHTS

*I have learned that if I want your
attention all I have to do is to knock over
or take one of David's toys.*

David gets to go to gymnastics and swimming. You and I go and watch him. David gets to play in the front yard by himself, I have to have a grown-up with me when I'm in the front yard. David gets all the attention and the good things. So today when we were in the family room I knocked over David's tower. He hit me on the arm, I screamed, and you came running. Then David got in trouble and had to go to time-out in his room. Now I have you all to myself, David hurt me, please cuddle with me and make me feel better. I love to cuddle. This works every time. You say "David, you are the oldest and you should know better." Bye, David, I have Mom all to myself.

You dreamed when I was born about how David and I would be best friends one day, playing together nicely. I can see how frustrated you get when David and I fight. We fight a lot, mostly over toys.

> Give David and me each a place
> for our special toys.

I don't want David to touch my cars. They are mine, and I will grab it away from him if he has one. Having things that are mine is very important to me. I am becoming an independent person and those cars are a part of me. Please give me a box for my cars and other special treasures. David could have a box for his, too. Then you could tell us that we don't have to share what is in our box if we don't want to. We may need a box for sharing toys, too. Some of our toys don't belong to just David or to just me.

Letting me have things of my own will help but not stop all the fighting. You see I am just learning about ownership, and sometimes I think that anything I want is mine. That's why I put up such a fuss when David won't let me play with his boat. Even though I saw him get it as a birthday present, I like it so much I want it to be mine. You will need to remind me (several times) that it is David's boat. I will scream because I really want it. You might be tempted to make David let me play with it, but if you do I will continue to see it as mine instead of beginning to learn that other people have special possessions, too. Besides if you make David let me play with it, he will be so mad that he will take one of my cars or throw sand at me later in the sandbox.

Another thing that might help is if David had his own place to build his special structures where I couldn't knock them over. It's just so tempting when it's on the floor of the family room.

Help us solve our conflicts.

I like it when David gets in trouble. But we would probably fight less if you didn't always take my side. Sometimes I start the fight, other times David does. Most of the time I can't remember. If you helped us learn how to solve our problems then we could work on finding solutions instead of getting each other in trouble and getting revenge. If David and I both want to play with the pretend food from the sharing box, it would help if you said "I see two boys who both want to play with the food. How can we solve this problem?" I often don't see a solution, but David might. He is older. If neither of us has any ideas you could make some suggestions. As we get older and have more practice problem solving with you we will be able to find our solutions without having you around.

It's good to learn how to solve problems, but now I have a new problem. If you are no longer taking my side how will I get your undivided attention? I need to have time with just you when I don't have to share you with David. Have any ideas?

SIBLING (PREPARING FOR NEW BABY)

Mrs. Johnson asked me if I was excited about the baby. What baby? I'm your baby, why do you need another?

Why am I getting a new brother or sister? My friend Sam has a brother and Nick has a baby sister. He says all she does is cry and eat. What are we going to get? Where do you get babies? Will I get to be the big brother?

I'M NOT VERY SURE ABOUT THIS BABY THING. HERE ARE SOME THINGS THAT WILL HELP ME GET READY FOR THE BABY.

Reassure me that you love me.

You always say I'm your special baby boy. Did I do something wrong so now you're going to get a new baby? Will you still love me after the baby is born? I need to hear "You will always be my special baby boy. I have enough love for you and for a new baby." Let's cuddle and look at my baby pictures. Tell me again about how happy you were when I was born. I like that story.

I want to go with you to shop for the baby.

When everyone is talking about the baby and not talking to me, I get scared that you won't love me, only the baby. I can help you get ready for the new baby. That's what a big brother should do. I can pick out really good toys for the baby and help get the baby's room ready. I like hearing that I am a great helper.

Tell me about babies.

If I am going to be your helper I will need to know something about babies. I like the books from the library. Let's read again the one where the big brother is holding the baby. Maybe Nick's mom would let us visit his new baby sister. I would like to hold her. Nick says his baby sister cries a lot. Why do babies cry? If I had my own baby doll, I could pretend it was our new baby. When will our baby be able to play trucks with me?

Let me know what will happen
when the baby comes.

Are you sick? You're always going to the doctor's. When will we get our baby? How will it get out? What is a hospital? Can we go visit it? Who will take care of me when you are at the hospital? Let's pretend hospital. You are the mommy, this is the hospital, my doll is the new baby, and I'm the big brother. If we don't like the baby, can we take it back?

Sock Struggles

You think I am choosing to be difficult, I'm not. You are not listening, these socks don't feel right!

Every morning we have trouble. You put my socks on and I fuss. Most of the time you just insist I wear them. Some days you go get me another pair, but they don't feel good either. Socks make both of us crabby. Why do socks feel so bad? You wear socks, don't they feel bad to you? I want to wear my sandles, no socks.

IT WOULD HELP IF YOU WOULD:

Recognize that my skin is very sensitive to how socks feel.

We have a lot of problems over clothes, mostly because I want to decide what I will wear. But the problem with socks is different. Socks make my feet feel bad. So bad that it hurts when I run, jump, or even walk. Nothing makes me happy when my feet hurt. Please understand that I am not just being silly. This is really a problem.

163

Help me identify the problem.

I don't have the words to tell you what the problem is, so I fuss. Tell me "You are a boy with sensitive skin. Some clothes just don't feel good to you." It would help if I knew the words *bumpy, tight,* and *scratchy.* Then I could tell you that those big socks are too bumpy inside my shoe. My toes can't move in my yellow socks, they're too tight. And the worst are my lion socks, they're all scratchy and they have threads that catch. One pair of socks that doesn't feel so bad are my red socks, we can get them to lay down just right on my feet and there is no seam at the toe. I want to wear those red socks every day. I don't care if they're stinky. Maybe we should get some more like that.

Oh yeah, there are a few other things that bother me. I don't like scratchy pants or shirts that are tight around my neck or tags, like the one at the neck of my sweatshirt is really bad. But I love my blue sweatpants and green T shirt. They feel so soft and good.

SPANKING

Can I hit you or Timmy when I don't like what you do?

Sometimes you get so angry that you spank me. Don't do that, it hurts. You spanked me after I grabbed my truck from Timmy. It is mine, and I wanted it. I hate Timmy. When you spanked me at the store after I made a fuss about a cookie I was so mad all I could think of was hitting you back. Why can't I hit you?

Why don't you hit the other people at the store when you get angry or the paperboy when he is late? Or is it only okay to hit those who are smaller than you? Mark at day care is only one year old, sometimes he makes me really angry.

I'M CONFUSED. IS SPANKING OKAY OR NOT?

Why do you spank me?

When you spank me I get so upset that I don't think about why I was spanked. I don't think at all, I just feel. I feel helpless and afraid of you. I must be a bad person. Is that how I'm supposed to feel? Is that what you were trying to teach me?

Please find other ways to teach
me how to behave.

Being two can be really tough. I live in the moment and often don't remember things like don't pull the dog's tail, don't go into the street, and don't touch the plant. I have so many things to learn. It's all very confusing, one day I get a cookie at the grocery store and the next time you say no. I used my words to tell Timmy I want my truck and he says no. My friend Paul lives on the other side of the street, I like playing with him. I hear no all day long.

I don't want to be bad. I need you to help me, not hit me. Please show me what to do, not just tell me what not to do. Please put away things that I am not supposed to touch, it would make my life and yours so much easier. I am interested in everything and forget about which things I can touch and which I can't. I hope that when I'm three I'll be able to remember the nos better. Right now I need to be reminded a lot!

When I'm tired and hungry I have a hard time controlling my strong feelings. Spanking me doesn't help me get in control. I just get mad. I start screaming and I don't know how to stop. I want something but I don't know what. May I just want you. Please don't hit me, I just don't know. Saying "Mark, when you are tired and hungry you lose it" helps me to understand why I feel so bad. Going shopping is hard anyway, please don't take me when I am hungry or haven't had my nap. Sometimes I can be hard to be around, even I don't like being around me.

I have a hard time controlling myself when I am angry. Do you ever feel that way? When I'm kicking the counter or pulling the dog's tail don't yell over and over for me to stop from the kitchen. If I don't stop after the first no, come help me stop. I need that kind of help sometimes. Tell me that I may not pull the dog's tail. On those days when I really, really make you angry you might need to leave the room and take a few big breaths. When you feel a little better tell me "I get very angry when you hit your baby brother. It's not okay to hit." Then we could talk about what I can do when Timmy takes my toy and won't give it back.

TANTRUMS

Sometimes I just lose it. The feelings are so strong inside me that the only thing I can do is to throw myself on the floor and scream. It is pretty scary.

So many things set me off. Yesterday, for example, you turned off the TV before *Barney* was over. Wow, was I angry. Then I tried to put the pieces in the train puzzle and they wouldn't fit. After lunch Matthew had a friend come over and the two of them went into his room and shut the door. I'm big now and I want to play with the big kids. It had been a tough day and it wasn't even dinnertime and I was exhausted by nap time.

I can tell you get terribly upset, too, when I lose

it. But yelling at me to stop it only makes it worse. You see I am out of control, and I can't stop.

PLEASE DON'T YELL AT ME. TRY THESE INSTEAD:

Stay near me.

Being out of control is really frightening. Do not leave me alone. Sit near me and let me know that you are available to help me. Your gentle touch may help calm me after a few minutes.

Help me move on.

The first few minutes I'm so overwhelmed I can't hear your words. But words can help me to calm down after the initial outburst. With your calm voice say "You're angry because the boys won't let you play with them. You don't want to be left out. This is enough, it's time to find something else to do and I will help you." Then we could play in a sink of bubbles, dig in the sandbox, pound some Play-Doh, or have a pillow fight. All of these really help me get rid of my angry feelings.

Avoid my trigger points.

I love trains, but every time I play with the train puzzle I get so frustrated. Maybe you should put it up for a while until I'm more likely to be successful. And please don't turn *Barney* off, he is my favorite. I sometimes have trouble moving from one activity to the next. If you would wait until *Barney* was over it would be easier for me to come to breakfast.

Next time Matthew has a friend over, let me know ahead of time so that you and I can plan some time together. Maybe we could make some cookies. Yum!

Oh, yeah, don't forget that I do better shopping and running errands when I am well rested. I find these activities very tiring and can get easily over-whelmed. And when I'm hungry I really have trouble when things don't go the way I want them. Have you ever had that problem?

TELEVISION

I want to watch my animal video again.
I want to see the zebras running
from the lions.

If you turn on the television I will watch it. Animal shows are my favorite, but I will watch anything. I sit and cuddle with blanket. There are a lot of things on TV that I've never seen before and that I don't understand. So I like to see the same show over and over, I am trying to figure out what is going on. When I watch TV I don't do anything else.

I CAN SPEND A LOT OF MY DAY WATCHING TV. I NEED YOU TO DECIDE HOW MUCH TV IS GOOD FOR ME.

Watch TV with me.

When I watch TV by myself I don't have anyone to answer my questions. Why is the little girl sad? Will she be okay? Why is the bear eating the honey? Will the bees sting the bear? I learn a lot by watching television. I learn about junk food, toys to buy, and hurting people. I also learn about animals

171

and sharing. I don't know good from bad on TV. I like it when you are with me and we can talk about what I see. I depend on you to know what is right and what is best for me.

Turn the TV off.

I like television. It is full of colors and sounds and noises. You seem to like it, too. When you're busy you turn it on and tell me to go watch some TV. But I also like to go down my slide, shoot my ball into the basket, and drive my cars. When the TV is on a lot I don't have enough time to do these things. It would be good if we watched the animal show after I wake up and then turned the TV off. I may fuss, I'm used to watching a lot of TV, and it's hard to let go. It would help if you spent a few minutes with me setting my train up or let me help you make the salad. I have been so busy watching, I need your help to get busy doing.

THUMB SUCKING

I started comforting myself with my thumb before I was born, don't ask me to stop now during the really tough times.

You were gone for a long time today. I started to get upset a few minutes ago because I was tired and hungry, but then I cuddled with my blanket and put my thumb in my mouth. Linda said you would be home soon. With my blanket and my thumb I was able to get calm and wait.

I like it when you hold me and comfort me when I'm having a hard time. You worry that my thumb sucking is a sign that you aren't doing something right. That you aren't a good parent. But it is a two-year-old's job to become independent from his or her parents. I have to learn how to face my upset feelings by myself. It can be really scary and frustrating to be independent. I have more courage to try new things because I bring along a friend, my thumb.

YOU ARE A GREAT PARENT. PLEASE DON'T WORRY ABOUT MY THUMB SUCKING. INSTEAD TRY THIS:

Ignore my thumb sucking.

At times all my friends need something to help them feel better. My friend Jerome has a blanket, Melissa uses a pacifier, and Ryan twirls her hair. I've seen adults chew gum, smoke cigerettes, and bite their nails when they feel bad. Yelling at me to take my thumb out of my mouth only makes me feel more upset and need to suck on it more. Soon I will use my thumb for many other things. It's not as big a deal as lots of grown-ups seem to feel. I don't see my older friends sucking on their thumbs, so there must be a time when I won't need it anymore. Life must be easier when you're three and four.

TIME-OUTS

*NO! I don't want a time-out. No, no, no,
don't make me have a time-out!*

Ryan took my horse. When he sat the horse down
I grabbed it, and I grabbed the cow, too. Why is
Ryan crying? Please don't yell at me. I'm not a bad
boy. Don't make me go to my room and leave me
there alone. I'm feeling angry at Ryan, and when
you leave me I get scared. I won't stay in here, you
can't make me. If you hold the door closed I will
kick it and pound it. It feels so bad, I am out of
control. Do you still love me?

HERE'S HOW TO WORK WITH ME ON THIS:

Teach me skills.

I get so excited when I see Ryan. He and I are
friends. Sometimes we have problems, mostly
when he takes a toy I was playing with or knocks
over my blocks. When we start to have problems
you put me in time-out and tell me to think about
what I did. But I'm not sure. I am so upset about
going to time-out that I can't think about my problems with Ryan at all. I am just learning how to

175

play with other children. Ryan and I need you to help us learn to play together. We need words like "No, mine"; "Please, give it to me"; "Me, next"; "My turn"; "You hurt me."

Give me a break.

Sometimes when Ryan and I play I really have problems. At times it's because I'm angry or frustrated, but not always. Sometimes I just don't have the energy to stay in control. My insides get all jumpy and I hit Ryan or throw an animal at him, or knock over his toys or just run around the room. Please stop me before I get out of control. I need a break. It helps when you say "Miles, you are starting to have problems, let's go sit in the rocking chair for a few minutes until you feel better." Rocking with you helps. Other things that help me feel calm are reading a book, blowing bubbles, and washing my toys in bubbly water. Breaks are good, they help me to get the energy I need to play again. Do you ever feel like you could use a break?

Help me express my anger.

When I feel angry it fills up my whole body. Making me sit in a chair or stay on my bed doesn't work. I can't do it. How do I get rid of all this anger? Don't tell me not to be angry. I am. I need you to tell me that it is not okay to hit Ryan, but it is okay to be angry. Show me that I can show my anger by hitting the floor or my pillow with my hands. After all the angry feelings are gone, please give me a hug. Hugs really help.

TIMIDNESS

I don't want to go to Taylor's house, she hits me and takes my toys. You tell me not to hit other children, not to take their toys, not to scream. I try to be good, but other kids don't. It scares me, I don't know what to do.

I love my doll. I take her everywhere. We go to Taylor's house a lot. I like the toys at Taylor's house, but Taylor hurts me. Today I was just about to give my doll some birthday cake when Taylor hit me and grabbed my doll. I was so scared I just let go and started to scream. I wanted to say "Help! Taylor has my doll," but the words don't come, I just cry. I feel so weak.

I'm scared of other kids, too. Kids take my toys away a lot. Sometimes a grown-up goes to the other child and tells them that it is not okay to take my toy, then they take the toy and give it back to me. But sometimes the grown-up doesn't do anything. I don't know what to do or even what I am supposed to do. I try to be nice but that doesn't seem to help. Just leave me alone.

PLEASE HELP ME LEARN HOW TO HANDLE THESE TOUGH SOCIAL SITUATIONS.

Help me stand up for my rights.

I don't want anyone taking my doll from me. She is mine. Let me know that I don't have to let kids take toys from me. That I can look right at the other child and hold on tightly. And that I can use my words "No! My doll." Tell me that my strong voice works better in this situation than my quiet voice. Kids have to be strong without being mean. Learning this will also help me know good from bad.

If you see the other child grab my toy, come and see me first. I'm the one who is upset. Why should that child get all the attention. Give me some ideas about what I might do next. That way if there isn't a grown-up around I will have some ideas on what to do. Let's see, I could find another doll and offer her that doll.

Don't force me to be around really mean kids.

It's important that I learn to stand up for myself, but some kids are mean. Please don't make me be with them. I need to know that it is all right to choose to walk away from scary situations. There may come a time when leaving a situation is safer than standing up for myself. When I'm older, I will pick friends who play nicely and stay away from the mean ones. So please don't take me to Taylor's house. Maybe if we go to the park with her and her mommy it will be better.

TOILET TRAINING ACCIDENTS

*I'm sorry, I was excited that Mikela came
over to play and I just forgot to go
to the potty.*

Learning to use the potty is not as easy as you
think. You've been doing it a lot longer than I have.
Just because it's easy for you doesn't mean it's
easy for me. I want to go to the potty right, I just
don't know how. I'm confused. I can tell this is important to you so I am trying. For my whole life I
have only noticed being wet or poopy after it has
happened. Now you want me to know in time to tell
you, to go to the potty and to get my pants down.
Sometimes I don't feel when I need to go pee until
right before it happens. Then I run to the potty
only to pee on the floor because I can't get my
clothes off. Then I feel really sad because I know
that made you unhappy. At times I don't feel the
need to pee at all, like when I am busy playing or
really tired. I don't like to be wet, I don't like to be
a mess, please help me get clean.

LEARNING TO USE THE POTTY IS HARD WORK.
HERE'S HOW YOU CAN HELP:

Reassure me that accidents are okay.

Please don't get angry and yell or spank me. I just had an accident. I feel bad. I need to hear that acci-

dents happen, that next time maybe I'll make it to the potty. Don't make me stay wet as a punishment, help me get clean. Tell me I did a good job when I do pee in the potty, but don't get too excited. I get afraid that I won't always make it to the potty and that I'm a bad girl when I don't.

There are days when I just don't want to worry about making it to the potty. Give me the option of wearing a diaper. I promise I won't still be wearing one when I graduate from high school. I really don't want to wear one, but sometimes I just can't grow up that fast. Let me put a sticker on the calendar when I do use the potty. That way I can see my successes.

Teach me to listen to my body.

Tell me that my body gives me signals when it needs to go pee or poop. A kind of funny feeling in the tummy is a sign that I need to poop. When I get tight inside and cross my legs then I probably need to pee. If I feel either of these I should let you know and we can go to the potty together. I feel more confident when you are there. What did it feel like when you were a kid? How did you learn? Do you remember?

Please take me to the potty as soon as I tell you. I can't wait five or ten minutes until you go through the checkout line in the grocery store. I know you had just asked me if I needed to go a few minutes earlier when we were near the bathroom but I didn't need to go then. I need to go now. I NEED TO GO NOW . . . OOPS.

TOOTHBRUSHING

Stop it! It feels yucky, like I'm going to throw up.

You say it's time for toothbrushing. I say no! I want to decide what I'm going to do. I like to do fun things like play with my boat and cups in the bath, pound Play-Doh, and ride on my rocking horse. I choose things that make my body feel good. Toothbrushing feels so bad. I don't choose toothbrushing. It feels so bad that I hold my mouth shut and struggle to get away every time.

MY FAVORITE IDEA IS NO TOOTHBRUSHING. SOME OTHER IDEAS ARE:

Help me feel in control.

If I really have to brush my teeth, let me choose the toothbrush. And let me hold the toothbrush with you. You can tell me first we are going to start with the smiley teeth in the front. Then we will do the yawning teeth in the back. I think I want to choose if we do the smiley teeth or the yawning teeth first. Make me the offical teeth checker. When you finish brushing your teeth let me check to be sure they are sparkling clean. Explain why you have fillings in your teeth. I can check my own in the mirror. Let me have a special toothbrush for my stuffed dog, Amos. Dogs need to have their teeth brushed, too.

Make toothbrushing feel better.

Toothbrushing is scary, my mouth is full of stuff, and the brush is moving all around. Maybe if I went with you to the dentist, she could show us a gentler, less scary way to brush my teeth. She might let me choose a special toothbrush just for kids. And she might say it is all right if I brush my teeth all by myself in the morning and with a parent at night. When the dentist tells me I need to brush my teeth to keep them healthy I listen. I don't listen when you talk about toothbrushing because you are my parent and I'm working on becoming my own person, separate from you. I do this a lot. Have you noticed?

Toy Cleanup

You see a floor covered with toys, I see my train with an engine stopped at the station, my books waiting to be looked at, the cups and plates ready for a tea party, and an empty puzzle with pieces close by.

You want me to clean up my tea party before I start on this puzzle. But I'm not done with playing tea, I just saw this puzzle and I want to work on it for a few minutes. After that I might drive my train around the track or look at a book or maybe have some more tea. I feel so good when all my most favorite toys are out where I can see and touch them all. Don't grown-ups like to be surrounded by their favorite things?

You tell me to pick up my toys. Do you really want me to pick up all of them? There are so many toys I don't know where to begin. Please show me how.

I AM GOING TO NEED YOUR HELP WITH THIS. IT WOULD HELP IF YOU WOULD:

Be my toy-cleanup assistant.

Tell me that you are here to help with toy cleanup. You will tell me the first two jobs to be done and I get to choose which one you have to do. But don't give me too many choices. Okay, the choice is books or animals. You get to do animals, I'll do books. I like being able to tell you what to do. And I need you to break the jobs into small tasks. It's fun when we do it together.

Limit toy cleanup.

I need toys, time, and space to try out all my ideas. I don't see any reason for cleaning up. Cleaning up interferes with my play. Give me a place to play where my toys aren't in your way. Show me that some of my toys like books and puzzles can get hurt when they are left on the floor. Give me a container or a shelf where I can put them and still keep them close. And then help me get them.

Please don't make me put my train up at bedtime. I'm not done with it. I want to build a bridge, put some trees around it, and put a zoo in the middle. I am really into it right now. Think of it as a big project. Grown-ups don't like to clean up their projects before they're done either. If you just watch you will see when I'm done playing with my train and have moved on to something else. That's when I'm ready and willing to help you clean up my train.

TRANSITIONS

No! I don't want to come to lunch.
No bath! I don't want to get dressed!
I don't want to go!

I am not being stubborn. I am having trouble stopping what I am doing and starting something else. Imagine you were in the middle of a big project and all of a sudden a giant picked you up and carried you off to the bathroom demanding you take a bath. That happens to me all the time and all I can do is scream and kick. It's not that I don't like to take baths, I do. I like them so much that I start fussing when you tell me it's time to get out and get my clothes on. I don't like change, not when it's a surprise and when I don't have any say in it. There are too many changes during the day, it really tires me out.

CHANGES WOULD BE EASIER FOR ME IF YOU WOULD:

Warn me that change is coming
and help me stop.

Tell me before a change is coming what is going to happen. Sit down next to me and say "When the dancing with bears song is over it will be bath time" or "After you go down the slide two more times it will be time to come in for lunch." Then stay with me while I finish sliding and we can race into the house. Having you here helps me remember that change is happening soon. If you leave I'm likely to forget and then put up a fuss when you come out to get me. At bath time it helps when you ask me which of my animals I would like to take to the bath tonight. Then I can stop thinking about tapes and start thinking about my bath.

One of the hardest changes for me is when it is time to leave Liam's house. I have so much fun playing there and then you just come and want to go. I'm not ready to go. I need time to finish what I am doing. Please don't rush me, I hate to be rushed. Tell me that I will get to come back and see Liam again very soon and let me say bye, bye to Liam, to Liam's mom, and to Liam's cat.

Use routines.

We have problems every morning. Most mornings I get busy playing with my toys and then you sit down and start combing my hair. I fuss because you are bothering me, I am playing. You keep interrupting me for breakfast, day clothes, and then toothbrushing whenever you want. It would help if

I put on day clothes first thing when you're changing my diaper, then before I can get busy playing fix me breakfast. After breakfast we could do hair combing and toothbrushing. Draw me a picture of my important morning activities and ask me to show you what is next. "I know what is next, toothbrushing." Routines help me get through all the changes in the day.

Whining

No is not always the final answer, if I ask over and over again sometimes you let me have what I want.

This is my favorite store because they give cookies to children. When you put me in the shopping cart I say "Cookie, Mommy." When we ride down by the bananas I ask again "Cookie, Mommy." I have asked two times with no reply. Maybe you didn't hear me, so I change my tone. "Mommy, cookie." "Stop whining no cookie," you replied. But this is the cookie grocery store, and I want my cookie so I keep saying "want cookie." Finally, with an angry look on your face, you tell me I'm driving you crazy and we go to the cookie lady and I get my cookie. Thank you.

I DON'T WANT TO DRIVE YOU CRAZY, BUT I'M A LITTLE CONFUSED. I NEED YOU TO:

Help me to understand what whining is.

You tell me to stop whining, but I am not sure what whining is. I think it has something to do with my voice. Maybe we could use the tape recorder to tape my voice when I'm whining. We could tape my voice when I'm not whining and then listen to both.

Teach me ways to ask for things that won't hurt your ears.

You have told me what not to do, but now I need you to teach me what to do. How would you like me to ask for things? Would including "please" sound better? I could practice using my regular voice into the tape recorder.

I won't always remember this new way, so when I start to whine tell me to ask again in a more pleasant voice.

There may be times when I'm hungry or tired and trying to talk in my polite voice will be hard. On those days I will need a lot of patience and a hug. When I hear your whining voice I'll try to re-member that you're having a hard time and I will give you a hug.

Listen and respond to my requests.

Please stop and listen to my request. I will ask over and over until I get a response. If your answer is yes, tell me that right away so I don't have to whine to get one. When I can't have what I'm asking for tell me why. Maybe I could get a cookie and have it with dinner, since it's almost dinnertime. Next time we go to the cookie store, you could surprise me by going and getting my cookie first thing before I even ask. That would be really great.

HY

"Is today Saturday?" "No, today is Tuesday." "Why?" "Why is it raining?" "Why does the dog eat carrots?" "Why is Nicole crying?" "Why do I have brown eyes?" "Why did you say enough no more questions?"

Why is my best word, it makes things stop and it gets your attention. I love *why*. Why don't you like *why*? . . . Why? Right now I am spending all of my time finding out about things. There are so many things to know. Like what happens when I hide Champ's ball, and how many toys will my bucket hold and how high can I stack the blocks before they fall down. These are things I can learn about on my own. There are a lot of things I want to understand that I can't find out on my own. Like why did the toast burn and why do we have to go to the store and why do I need to learn to use the potty.

When I say *why*, you stop and talk to me, I like that. I try very hard to understand what you're saying, but most of the time I still don't get it, so then I say *why*. Even when I know the answer I sometimes say *why*. It makes me feel good to know that I knew that. And sometimes when you're ready to leave my room at night I ask a question so you will stay with me a little longer. I like *why* and so I use it a lot.

I AM TRYING TO LEARN ABOUT THINGS AROUND ME. HERE'S HOW YOU CAN HELP:

Answer my questions.

I have some ideas about why the toast burned, like the electricity in the wall was too hot. With your help I can know what really happened. If I got to put the toast in the toaster and watch it get hot, then I could see how bread becomes toast. Don't forget to tell me that I can make toast only when I have the help of a grown-up. Bread goes in the toaster, nothing else. I don't like surprises, so the more I know about the things around me the better I feel. If I don't know the reason, I'll imagine my own. When you say to me "You ask very good questions" I really feel good. It makes me want to learn even more. I will keep asking questions, learn new words, and come up with ideas about the world. I'm so excited about learning. Isn't that what you want?

I can tell that my excitement for learning sometimes makes you upset or tired. Please don't yell or ignore me. Aren't my ideas and questions important? If I can't rely on you to answer my questions now, what will I do when I get older and I have some really important questions? It's okay if you don't know the answer, maybe we could go to the library and get a book. If you're tired or need to do something else tell me "Katey, I have answered all the questions I can right now. No more questions until after dinner." Please understand if I ask, why?

Give me information.

You don't have to wait for me to ask questions. I like it when you tell me and show me about things. I've learned that police cars, fire trucks, and aide cars make a loud noise, so other cars will get out of their way. We have a book that shows lots of kinds of planes. We have planes fly over our house all the time. And I have learned that some of my toys are made of plastic and some of metal. The toys that are plastic can go in the bathtub and the toys made of metal can't. I learned how vanilla, sugar, and pumpkin smell when we made pumpkin muffins and then I got to eat them. Yum. Why do I like pumpkin muffins?